BEHIND THE CURTAIN OF THE BEAUTIFUL GAME

A COLLECTION OF SHORT STORIES TAKING YOU CLOSER TO THE CHARACTERS AND THE CHARM OF FOOTBALL ACROSS THE GLOBE

BY
CALLUM MCFADDEN

First Edition.
First published 2023

Published by:
Morgan Lawrence Publishing Services Limited
Ridge House Annexe
16 Main Ridge West
Boston
Lincolnshire
PE21 6QQ
www.morganlawrence.co.uk
email: info@morganlawrence.co.uk
Company number: 12910264

A CIP catalogue record is available for this book from the British Library.

Cover design by LCgrapix.

Printed and bound in Bulgaria by Pulsio Print.

Dedication

To my beautiful wife and my best friend, Mary-Ann. Thank you for supporting me in this project as you do each and every day of my life.

To my mum, Maria. Thank you for taking me to football as a kid, looking after me and bringing me up to be an adult who I hope can always make you proud.

To my sister, Michelle and my niece, Eva. Thank you for your support and love and for always making me laugh.

For my late dad, Hugh. I wish you were alive today to read this book and see all the things that I have achieved in life so far.

Contents

Tribute to Craig Brown

During the process of putting together this book, one of my biggest supporters and a contributor to this book, Craig Brown passed away.

Craig was a colossus of Scottish football and managed Scotland to the World Cup in 1998 which remains the last World Cup we have qualified for.

He played for one of the greatest Dundee teams in history in the 1960s. At Dens Park, he won the Scottish league title in 1962 and reached the semi-final of the European Cup before turning his hand to teaching and football management.

He started his career in management at Scottish lower-league side Clyde FC while being a primary school headteacher. I once asked him what was the most challenging of those roles to which he replied: "Managing the team was similar to managing the school in many ways except the school was probably more challenging but both were rewarding."

Rewarding was what time in Craig's company was.

When I first started out interviewing former players and managers, I was speaking to people at a local level and, rather ambitiously, I reached out to Craig asking to speak to him.

Bearing in mind Craig was a man who had managed at club level in Scotland and engaged and led his country while alongside people like Sir Alex Ferguson, Walter Smith, Kenny Dalglish and many others, I fully expected him to politely decline. Even more so, given that I had about five interviews behind me and he would not have had the slightest clue who I was.

However, that was not to be the case. I received a reply from Craig saying that he would be more than happy to speak to me and that we should arrange a call.

This was during the first COVID-19 lockdown, so our chat was to be over Zoom. I fully expected a short fifteen-minute chat which I would have been over the moon with before saying goodbye and thanks to Craig.

That was not his style. We were on the call for over three hours and we spoke even after when we had stopped recording, with Craig asking about my background and my family while telling me to stay in touch.

He gave me his phone number and we stayed in touch with him helping me with contacts for future interviews and general chats about football and life.

He was a gentleman in every sense of the word. Humorous and talkative yet humble and grounded. He showed as much interest in those he met as they did in him.

When I started my own football website in 2020, he would read my articles and told me he would help me in any way that he could.

I joked that I would love to have him write a column given his experiences in the game and he said yes straight away.

He told me that he would send me his columns on a Sunday evening and that I could publish them whenever I wanted to during the week.

Again, everything done with kindness, empathy and enthusiasm.

I was fortunate to meet him at Celtic versus Aberdeen last year and it was great to spend time speaking to him and thanking him for his help, particularly when I was starting out with no track record.

"We all have to start somewhere but remember me when you are moving up in the world," was the response with a smile.

That was Craig Brown in a nutshell. He always made you feel on top of the world with his charm and wit.

With those qualities, it is no surprise to me that he achieved so much in the game for club and country.

He will be sorely missed by all who knew him and all who follow Scottish football.

FOREWORD
BY DANIEL GEEY

Callum and I first spoke in December 2019. He wanted to be a football journalist but had not been able to land a job after finishing university. It soon became clear that he had a great grasp of the sports and football space. It turned out for decades he read for hours each day about the industry. I challenged him to start blogging. He sent me a first draft the very next day.

As an aspiring teacher, he already had an excellent writing style and his CFB football blog then very quickly evolved into a global podcast series with high-profile guests and a huge reach.

Callum had no idea of the opportunities that were ultimately waiting for him. He has interviewed global sports superstars and his football network has blossomed as a result. His proactivity led him to become one of the top Scottish football podcast platforms as well as working for his boyhood club Celtic.

It has been a real privilege to watch Callum grow from strength to strength, amplifying his voice as one of the up-and-coming content creators in Scottish and international football. His acceleration into the profession has been nothing short of remarkable and is an inspiration to many others who are looking to make inroads into the sports and football industry.

Your dad would be very proud pal.

INTRODUCTION
A lifelong love of the beautiful game

Football is sometimes referred to as 'only a game' usually by those who do not follow the sport closely. For me, I can genuinely say that football is one of the most important things in my life. Without being too philosophical, my wife Mary-Ann, my mum, my close family, friends, and football are the things that make me tick.

I've had ups and downs in my life as we all do, and I have struggled with bouts of depression since my father passed away when I was fourteen. However, throughout any struggle or strife that I have experienced, I can safely say that football has always been the escapism that gives me joy when the going gets tough as well as those closest to me.

The thrill of a Saturday is more than just watching a game of football. It's meeting up with friends, going on supporters' buses and the smell of the food vendors as you approach the stadium. Buying the match programme, settling into your seat, and hearing that rush of noise as your team emerge looking for an ever important three points. That is Saturday 3pm.

That is why we love football and that is what we as football fanatics desperately need in the routine of our lives.

Like many young boys and girls, I would always be kicking a football around the garden or the house from a young age. Transfixed from watching my first World Cup in 2002 – won by Brazil in Japan and South Korea – I even gave myself the nickname Caldo Ronaldo Ronaldinho Rivaldo.

That is how fascinated I was by the beautiful winning football of Brazil. Those greats and their impact on my love of the game remains to this day. Thankfully, that self-appointed nickname did not last...

I have always loved the characters within football – on and

off the pitch – and I dreamed of being a football writer and broadcaster when I was younger.

When I left secondary school, I had the grades to apply for sports journalism at university although I eventually decided to go down another academic route after family members emphasised how tough it can be to break into such an industry.

I honestly thought that my chances of ever having the opportunity to write and broadcast about football had gone when I did not pursue journalism at an academic level. However, after a horrendously tough battle with depression in 2019, I started to blog and podcast about football via my own small platform online.

Remarkably and much to my shock and surprise, things have grown quickly, and I have had the opportunity to speak to over four hundred professional footballers, managers, and members of the wider football community.

I now have a publisher in *World Football Index* who support my work, I commentate for the visually impaired supporters at my beloved Celtic and I hold a domestic UK press card and worldwide press card. All of which are well beyond my wildest dreams.

I have made many friends within the football industry including Manchester United icon Willie Morgan is now a close friend of my family and I. We work together fortnightly on a show together and it is the privilege of my life to work with Willie as well as each and every footballer, manager, staff member and journalist who has given me the time of day now and hopefully will continue to do so into the future.

Anyway, that is enough about me, I have always wanted to write a book which has led me to put pen to paper on this project. The aim of the book is simple. I want to take you as the reader behind the curtain of the beautiful game by sharing insight from icons of football, writers, commentators, and fans who make the game what it is.

All profits from this book will be donated to mental health charity 'Man On Inverclyde' because they make such a positive impact in my home region of Inverclyde. I have also benefitted from their support, and I want to give something back to anyone out there who is struggling. Please remember that you are never alone, and help is always available.

Football is my passion and I hope to be able to share that with you via the work that I have put into every single page of this book. Enjoy!

CHAPTER ONE
Playing the game

Norman Whiteside
The World Cup record breaker

Belfast born Norman Whiteside made over two hundred appearances for Manchester United and Everton, before a knee injury ended his career prematurely at just twenty-six years of age.

During his spell at Old Trafford, Whiteside won two FA Cups (1983 and 1985) and one Charity Shield (1983). He was also capped thirty-eight times by Northern Ireland and played in two World Cups (1982 and 1986).

You became Manchester United's youngest player since Duncan Edwards when you made your debut for the club in 1982. What was it like being a young player training and playing with the Manchester United first team?

It all happened very quickly for me. I went to a Home International open day at Old Trafford at the age of 15. Northern Ireland were a player short on the day and Sammy McIlroy said to the organisers that Whiteside is in the stand and would be able to play. Then, before I knew it, someone came up to the stand to get me and take me down to the dressing rooms to play for Northern Ireland in the tournament.

Incredibly, we went on to win the tournament and I performed very well. I had a skinhead at the time and no one knew who I was but that was the start of my journey with the club as I was signed there and then.

I didn't train with the first team a lot after being signed in all honesty. So, it was a shock for me when I got called up to the first team. Big Ron [Atkinson] asked me if I had a suit and when I replied yes, he told me to go and get it as I would be travelling with the first-team squad to Brighton. This was when teams could only use one substitute, so I didn't expect to get on and that was the first that I had heard of any first-team opportunities at the club.

I went down to Brighton and was named as a substitute as expected. I did not expect to come on, but Mike Duxbury pulled up injured and on I went to make my debut two weeks before my seventeenth birthday. I played twelve minutes in the game, but it felt great to get on at all.

The lasting memory that I have from that time was that I was earning £16 per week. On the night, we won the game with a goal from Ray Wilkins and the senior players started winding me up on the bus about what I would do with my win bonus. I was confused as I didn't even know what a win bonus was, or that we had a win bonus. They told me that our win bonus was £800 and I could not believe it. I went from earning £16 per week and travel expenses to earning £800 for twelve minutes work! It still makes me laugh to this day. That was the start of my career.

I kept my place in the team for the next two weeks and we won both of those games as well. That meant that I had earned £3,200 in win bonuses in my first three weeks in professional football. What makes it even better is the fact that I was not able to receive the money until my seventeenth birthday. It is fair to say that won't forget my seventeenth birthday as that was a nice bonus to receive.

All of the senior players at the club looked after me well. Sammy McIlroy was especially good with me and I think that was because we were both from Northern Ireland. If I needed anything then he would always help me. For example, as many teenagers do, I had a bit of a rash on my face and Sammy went and got me face cream from the chemist that would best help it. He even gave me his Northern Ireland jersey as a gift which meant a lot.

In the dressing room, I couldn't have sat between two more different people. On my left was Martin Buchan and on the right was Lou Macari. That was some introduction to the first-team dressing room and both looked after me.

You won two FA Cups while at Manchester United and scored in both cup final successes. What were those occasions at Wembley like to play in and how proud are you of scoring in those games?

I was lucky to be able to have success at Wembley. I scored in two semi-finals and in three cup finals there. I scored with my right foot, left foot and with a header in those cup finals. A perfect hattrick. When you are eighteen, you take cup finals in your stride as you think that you'll be playing in them every single year.

In the first FA Cup final against Brighton (1983), we should have lost in all honesty. We won the replay easily [4-0] and I scored the second goal in the game. That goal still stands, making me the youngest goal scorer in FA Cup final history. You play football to win things and, thankfully, I was able to win the FA Cup again two seasons later.

You played alongside many top players including Bryan Robson while at United. What was Bryan like to play alongside because as a captain he led by example?

Bryan was the best player in the country. He stood out for Manchester United and for England. We used to have a good rapport when I moved into midfield. He was the all-round midfield player. He could tackle, he could head the ball, he could pass, he could score and he could move from box to box with ease. He could do it all. You don't get players like him anymore.

He was the greatest player of that generation at United and captained the side for thirteen years. Roy Keane then followed Robbo a few years later and he was very similar for twelve seasons. Manchester United are very privileged to have had two of the best midfielders of their generation for twenty-five years.

I always enjoyed playing alongside Robbo. If anyone left a bad tackle on me then he'd swap position with me and get them back twice as hard. He was the England captain, so he got away with murder!

The fans at Old Trafford still sing your name to this day. What are your personal highlights from your time at Old Trafford and what does the club mean to you even today?

I love the club. I've worked at the club in a hospitality capacity for twenty-seven years in addition to my eleven years as a player. I've had thirty-eight years of association with the club and I still love going to Old Trafford each week. I loved my time at the club from day one and it meant a lot to my family as they were Manchester United fans.

I was not a Manchester United fan as a kid. I did not support any particular team, but I knew that I wanted to be a professional footballer more than anything else. I used to fly over and play for the junior side on a Saturday afternoon, watch the first team then fly home. That was my routine for six months before I then signed permanently for the club at sixteen. It was a big move to leave home for Manchester, but you are joining one of the biggest and best clubs in the world which makes it all worth it.

The club have me a guarantee at the age of fifteen of a one-year apprentice contract followed by a three-year professional contract, so they looked after me and helped me settle into life in Manchester.

Last but not least, you represented Northern Ireland on thirty-eight occasions, scoring nine goals as well as winning the Home Championship in 1984. You were also the youngest player since Pele to play at a World Cup. How would you sum up your international career?

It started off incredibly well by becoming the youngest player to ever play at the World Cup in Spain '82. I was seventeen years and forty-one days old. It was unbelievable for me from a publicity perspective. The scenes at the hotel for me were similar to the scenes years later when David Beckham signed for LA Galaxy. I was mobbed at the hotel.

Pele even sent me a video to wish me well. In the video, he said: 'I hope you are as successful as me at World Cups.' That made me laugh as I thought, I'm sure I'll have a chance of winning three World Cups. Thank you very much for that, Pele!

It was lovely to receive the message and the record still exists to this day. If no one breaks the record at the next World Cup in Qatar then I'll have been the youngest player for half of the World Cups in history. That would be a nice box to tick.

I'm very proud of that and of every opportunity that I had to play for the national team. It ended early for me due to injury which meant I couldn't add to my thirty-eight caps, but I played in two World Cups and played against Brazil before things slowed down for me in my mid-twenties.

*****

Nigel Quashie
Football and mental health

Nigel Quashie made his Premier League debut for QPR in 1995 aged seventeen and went on to make over fifty appearances for the Rs. Quashie also played for Nottingham Forest, Portsmouth, Southampton, West Brom, West Ham, Birmingham City, Wolves, and MK Dons, before returning to Loftus Road in 2010.

He was an integral member of the Portsmouth side that won the First Division championship in 2003 and he also won promotion with Birmingham in 2009.

Quashie represented Scotland on fourteen occasions, scoring one goal.

You came through the youth system at QPR and made your debut in 1995 at Old Trafford under the late Ray Wilkins. What are your memories of that special moment?

I was on the old YTS scheme and as part of that scheme, you had to go on an away trip and work with the kit man. I was lucky enough to be told that I would doing my duty at Old Trafford, so I travelled with the first team and thought nothing else of it. I helped make the teas and coffees on the coach and helped make sure all the kit and boots were there at the hotel the night before the game.

The following day, I was fully expecting to be putting out in the changing room pre-match but when the team was named, I was in it. I could not believe it. It was a surreal feeling, but Ray put me at ease and told me to go out and enjoy myself and treat the game as if I was playing at the park with my friends. I was grateful for the chance that he gave me, and he helped kickstart my career.

To showcase the mark of the man, he made sure that my mum

got to Old Trafford to watch my debut. He arranged all the travel and tickets to make sure she could watch my debut and he made sure that I was able to speak to her after the game. I was in shock at just how special he made what was already an incredible day for me. I will never forget Ray and how he treated me.

You established yourself in the first team at QPR over the next few seasons which led to interest from Nottingham Forest. You signed for Forest in 1998 and were at the club for two seasons. How do you reflect on your time there?

A lot of people do not know what my circumstances were when I was at Nottingham Forest. Some people thought it may have been due to the managerial change that my game time decreased but it was nothing to do with that. I had to deal with a painful personal issue that was the death of my son.

I got to the point where I never knew how to deal with such trauma at a young age myself. I had a big money move to Forest and people aren't aware that I was dealing with a situation that I would not wish on anybody. I had to try and overcome it, but I was in a really difficult situation and football was the last thing on my mind.

The only reason that I kept going as a footballer was due to a call from Tony Pulis. He called me one day and I did not know Tony, so I did not know why he was calling me. I answered the phone, and he asked me to come down to Portsmouth – where he was the manager – for a chat. I thought it was a long way to go for a chat, but he insisted.

He told me that he knew of my personal situation, that he wanted me to forget about football and that he had someone that he wanted me to talk to. I couldn't believe that someone who I did not know wanted to help me in such a way but having heard about my circumstances, his natural reaction was to try and help.

He introduced me to a sports psychologist and encouraged me to fully open up about how I felt and what I was going through. I did and it was such a great help to me. If it wasn't for him then I wouldn't have played football again. It really was the last thing on my mind. He was key to me overcoming my situation and like Ray, I will never forget what he did for me.

You signed for Tony Pulis's Portsmouth in 2000 after meeting him and reaching out to the sports psychologist that he arranged for you. What was your time at Portsmouth like as a whole?

I enjoyed my time at Portsmouth. Tony got me the help that I needed and told me that when I was ready that he wanted to help kickstart my career. He put no pressure on rushing me back into football but when I was ready to play again, he signed me and put his faith in me. He told me that he did not want me to worry about tactics or formations but to get back on the pitch and enjoy my football again without any unnecessary pressure. He gave me the freedom to be myself again and get my love for the game back, as well as get my life back on track too.

Following on from Tony, Harry Redknapp came in as manager and he was clear from the outset that he wanted to get the club promoted to the Premier League. If you weren't with him on that then he would move you on and he did that to several players. He brought in some unbelievable players to stamp their mark at the club such as Paul Merson and Robert Prosinecki. They could have a massive impact on any game, and I was grateful to be able to play with such players and play under Harry in a successful team.

We had high standards as a team and every player no matter of their stature pulled in the same direction. Portsmouth was full of great people and every player was willing to sacrifice themselves for the good of the team whenever required.

Winning promotion to the Premier League by playing the attractive football that we did was amazing. It was an unbelievable achievement for the club, but Harry was a great man manager, and he was the perfect man to take the club forward because he was a players' manager. The way that he was as a man made you want to play for him and do all that you possibly could to succeed for him and the club.

You had played in the Premier League in the 1990s but by the time you got there again, with Portsmouth in the mid-2000s, high levels of finance were coming into the league. Was it even more of a challenge than previously for you, given the players that clubs could attract throughout the league?

Absolutely. I was fortunate to see the progression of the Premier League year on year throughout my time playing in the top flight. As you say, more money coming into the league attracted world-class players which in turn improved the standard of the league as a whole. The games were quicker when I was at Portsmouth and the level of fitness that you needed was on another level to before.

The league has continued to grow year on year since I retired and success breeds success and that is what we are seeing in the Premier League of today.

Harry Redknapp moved from Portsmouth to bitter rivals Southampton in 2004. You followed him by making the same move. It was a controversial move at the time for you and him. How did you handle such pressure?

It was a strange situation for me because Portsmouth offered me a three-year contract to stay at the club which I accepted and was happy to sign. Then, Harry left suddenly, and my contract was withdrawn which I did not understand because I would have committed to Portsmouth regardless of Harry being the manager at the time.

Velimir Zajec took over from Harry and made it clear to me that I wouldn't be involved under him which confused me as I was a regular at the club. He told me that he was instructed by the powers that be not to play me which was hard to take. Within days of Zajec taking over, I was told that I was being sold and that I would not play if I stayed but instead be left to rot in the reserves.

A few clubs came in for me, but Southampton made the highest offer, and it was made clear to me that they were selling me to Southampton. It was a strange one, but I felt like I had no choice but to join Harry at Southampton.

You were at Southampton for eighteen months before joining Bryan Robson at West Bromwich Albion. What was it like to work with such a legend of English football?

Bryan was another great human being. He was clear on what he wanted me to bring to the team, but he also emphasised that I had to look after my mental health given the trauma that I had been through earlier in my life. He was a family-oriented man, and he was always about the players. Looking after you and getting the best out of you was his priority. As soon as he called me, I knew I wanted to play for him.

The supporters were great with me, and they still are to this day. I have a great connection with the club to this day and I have nothing but fond memories of the Albion.

You represented Scotland on fourteen occasions scoring one goal against Trinidad and Tobago. What did it mean to you to represent Scotland?

It was amazing for me and my family. My grandfather was Scottish, and my mum's side of the family are McFarlanes who are proud Scots. Berti Vogts was good with me, and the fans took to me too.

I am devastated that injury prevented me from having the opportunity to earn more caps because it was such a source of pride to pull on the jersey. I was never the same after my ankle injury, but I am proud of what I achieved across my career and particularly with Scotland.

*****

Matt Le Tissier
One club man

Nicknamed 'Le God' by Southampton fans, Matt Le Tissier spent his entire sixteen-year career with the Saints, making over four hundred appearances and scoring more than one hundred and sixty goals.

Le Tissier won eight caps for England.

You are an icon at Southampton having spent your entire career with the club. You are also a member of the illustrious one hundred club of the Premier League era alongside some of the greatest players to ever play in England. What are your personal highlights from your football career?

I won Player of the Year at the club three times which no other player has ever done in Southampton history so that stands out for me. That is a pretty cool thing to have next to my name.

I was also top scorer for the club in seven or eight seasons while I was at the club despite not being an out and out striker. I look back on that with pride.

Of course, I can't forget, scoring the last ever goal at the Dell. That was such a special moment for me because the Dell was such an important place in my career and in the history of the club.

Another stand out memory would be defeating Liverpool 4-1 in 1989 when they were one of the best sides in the country. It could have been seven or eight that day.

Those would be the highlights for me.

Being a one club man affords you legendary status at the club and always will do. How does that make you feel?

It fills me with great pride that I was able to contribute in such a big way to the football club. During my time at the club, we were never relegated despite having the lowest budget in the league for pretty much the whole time that we were there.

Even twenty years after I have retired, I still get a great reception from the fans which is a fantastic feeling.

You were given a special award by Athletic Bilbao in recognition of being a 'one club man' in 2015. What was that experience like for you and your family?

I was contacted by the club and their committee who had the idea of giving out this award.

To be chosen as the first person to receive the award was an incredible honour for me. They treated me and my family like royalty.They flew my wife and I over to Bilbao, looked after us for a couple of days and we were invited to watch the match between Bilbao and Real Sociedad.

At half time during that game, I was invited on to the pitch to receive the award. They showed a compilation of my best goals to the Bilbao fans on the big screens and the reception that they gave me as fantastic. It was a lovely moment.

Funnily enough, the Real Sociedad manager at the time was David Moyes so I was able to have a chat with him that day as well.

It was a day that I will never forget and I am grateful to Bilbao for the award and to their fans for their welcome.

There was a lot of interest in you during your career from clubs such as Tottenham, Liverpool and Chelsea. Did you ever come close to leaving and do you ever regret not moving on?

I have no regrets at all about staying at Southampton. It is my club and I loved every minute playing there. I would not swap it for anyone.

I nearly signed for Spurs in 1990 when I was 21 and had just won the PFA Young Player of the Year award but I changed my mind at the last minute when Terry Venables was manager. My agent also told me he had been in contact with Chelsea, Liverpool and Monaco around the same time as Tottenham too.

That was the closest I ever came to leaving. It got close, very, very close, to the point where we had agreed on wages and I had signed a document that would come in to force if the clubs agreed a fee during the summer break of that season.

But, in the end, Southampton gave me a new contract and offered me just as much as Tottenham had.

It was probably the hardest decision I had to make because of my loyalty as a Spurs fan but by this time I had settled on the South Coast and loved the club and the people down here. That was enough to keep me here.

Chelsea also tried to tempt me when my childhood hero Glenn Hoddle was their manager.

My agent rang me up and said 'Glenn Hoddle wants to buy you. Will you speak to him?' I said 'no.' I didn't want to have the conversation because I liked it at Southampton and the way I lived my life didn't really suit the bright lights of London.

Given that Terry and Glenn then went on to manage England, perhaps turning them down was not the best decision as far as my international career went.

In regard to your England career, you won eight caps which many football fans and pundits alike still question to this day given your undoubted ability. Do you believe that staying at Southampton rather than playing for a so called 'big' club contributed to the number of caps that you won?

It definitely played a part and thankfully, for the modern day players, I don't think it is as bad today as it once was.

In the 1990s, it was definitely a disadvantage if you were not at one of the bigger clubs. If I had been playing at Liverpool, Manchester United or one of the big London clubs and scoring the volume of goals from midfield that I was scoring then I am sure it would have been different.

I scored twenty-five goals in 1994 and followed that up with thirty goals in the following season yet I was still left out of squads at that time. If I had scored those number of goals at a bigger team then I'd probably have been one of the first names on the team sheet.

One of the greatest footballers of all time Xavi Hernandez has singled you out as being his footballing hero growing up. Given that he has won all that there is to win in football for both club and country, how does it feel to have that respect from a true footballing icon?

That was a very proud day for me because to have someone of his stature say such nice things about me was pretty amazing. That was nice moment and one that is unique.

I also had a moment in a pre-season friendly in the early 1990s when Southampton played against Juventus that was equally special.

We were warming up before the game and Gianluca Vialli - who was an icon of Italian football during that era - made the effort to stop his warm up with Juventus to come over to me and ask me if he could have my shirt after the game.

That was another unbelievable moment. I remember thinking 'Oh my God, this is Gianluca Vialli and he is asking me for my shirt. It should be the other way around.'

Those little moments are great to look back on and mean a lot.

You played football during the era of the old First Division and in the early Premier League years. Would you swap playing in your era of football for the chance to play in modern day game if you could?

The money is very different now and the chance to play on absolutely incredible pitches that are like carpets would be tempting compared to the money we earned and the state of some of the pitches that we played on.

However, to be honest, I would not swap my era for the money and the facilities of the modern day because I loved the era that I played in.

It was relaxed and you could still have a life outside of football as well as having a close relationship with the fans without worrying about camera phones and being pestered too much.

I wouldn't swap my time in the game for the world.

*****

Willie Morgan
Playing under an iconic manager and facing iconic players

A talented winger, Willie Morgan began his career in 1963 at First Division Burnley. Ironically, his first two Burnley goals came in a 6-1 victory over Manchester United, the club he signed for in 1968.

Morgan went on to make over two hundred appearances for the Red Devils and captained the side to the Second Division title in 1975. After leaving Old Trafford, Morgan played for Burnley, Bolton and Blackpool, and spent two seasons in America.

Morgan represented Scotland twenty-six times, including the 1974 World Cup.

You played under Sir Matt Busby at Manchester United. What it like for you as a humble boy from Sauchie in Scotland to play for him and then become a lifelong friend of his?

I played for the biggest club in the country, and I was very proud to have Sir Matt Busby pay a record fee for me at the time, and it was a wonderful time.

Sir Matt Busby was the best manager to ever grace the game in my opinion. He was a very special human being. He built one of the great club teams and it was like playing for your dad. He commanded the utmost respect without saying anything, and he was such a lovely guy.

I remember if we would lose a game he would say 'you did your best, have a nice weekend,' and it made you feel a thousand times worse because you did not want to let him down. You wanted to play well so that he would be proud of you.

We played a lot of golf together for many years afterwards and our families also got on well with each other. We would holiday together in Tenerife and stay on the same complex in Los Cristianos on the Costa Del Sol. I remember we played golf at a course called The Mere where he got his only ever hole in one at the twelfth hole, and I have a photograph of him being presented with his tie, as you receive a tie to mark the achievement.

Just playing at Old Trafford and just walking out before the game started with an atmosphere that was phenomenal, and to this day the supporters give excellent support to people like me. We were just happy to play football and get paid for it and things just happened, whereas clubs now are taking players and coaching them from four years old.

You also represented the Scotland national team on twenty-six occasions. What are your main memories of representing Scotland and what did it mean to you and your family?

I am just a normal working-class boy from Sauchie, so having the opportunity to play for Scotland was fantastic. I can honestly say that playing for Scotland one day was not something I dreamed about growing up because I never imagined that it would be possible. My dad worked down the pits and that was always the most likely outcome for me if it was not for football.

I have to say that when I first walked out at Hampden, the fans were incredible with me. I felt as if I was ten feet tall. It meant so much to me but also so much to my father. He loved nothing more than seeing me represent Scotland.

I returned to Hampden in 2022 to receive a silver medal for surpassing twenty-five Scotland caps during my playing career due to the decision to reclassify several tour matches that I played in 1967 as full international fixtures. That was a nice moment as I was presented the medal by SFA president Rod Petrie and Chief Executive Ian Maxwell. The only disappointment for me was not getting the medal presented to me on the Hampden pitch as I would love to have shared that moment with the Scotland fans because they always treated me so well. They are unbelievable fans who back the team no matter what.

What is your personal highlight from your time playing with Scotland?

My highlight has to be playing a big part in helping us qualify for the World Cup in 1974. I remember the game that we sealed qualification against Czechoslovakia like it was yesterday. I crossed the ball to assist Joe Jordan who scored the goal to take us to the World Cup. I can still picture it all in my head as we speak. I got the ball on the right wing, beat my full back and saw Joe making the run into the box. I crossed the ball with the outside of my right foot and the next thing I knew, Joe had scored. The noise of Hampden crowd and the feeling it gave me was amazing. You do not often experience highs like that. It was surreal. An unforgettable moment for sure.

You were one of the best wingers in British football as was Jinky Johnstone of Celtic. You did not play together for Scotland often. Do you think you could have played in the same team or were you too similar?

Of course we could have. Great players can always play together. I could've played on the left wing which I did at Manchester United from time to time.

Don't forget, George Best and I were able to play together successfully so Jinky and I wouldn't have had a bother. With Bestie, we would switch wings throughout games which always kept defenders alert. If Bestie was having a problem with the right back, he'd give me a shout and we'd switch and vice versa. Jinky and I could easily have done that too.

Jinky lining up on one wing with me on the other would have

been a scary thought for defenders of any team. We would take players on, assist plenty and score goals too. It is just a shame we were not given the opportunity on a regular basis.

What is your view on the modern game?

The modern game is ruined by coaches. They focus too much on trying to show how clever they are rather than letting players play. Don't forget, players win games of football, not coaches. Too much coaching turns players into robots. Where are the great wingers of the modern game for example? They just do not exist anymore.

Players now are coached to play safe or relentlessly keep possession rather than looking to score as many goals as possible like we did when I played. It is the same with young kids. I hate hearing about young kids being coached. That is madness for me because you have to let kids play and express themselves. Ask any kid in the playground and they'll tell you who can play. They don't need coaching at that age. The best will always showcase that naturally.

Given your view of the modern game, who do you believe is the greatest footballer of all time and are there any modern-day players who you rate highly?

For me, the greatest player of all time is Pele, without a shadow of a doubt. He is out on his own for me. I played against him in America when I played over there, and he was phenomenal. He actually had his own dressing room which he invited me into after our game against the Cosmos who he played for.

We swapped shirts and it felt amazing to have a match-worn Pele shirt such was my admiration for him. Unbelievably, I gave it to a young American player in the dressing room who told me how much it would mean to him to have it. Only I could give a shirt like that away (laughs) but meeting the great man and playing against him will always stay with me.

There is only one modern player who comes close to Pele and that is Lionel Messi. He is often compared with Cristiano Ronaldo which I find strange because Ronaldo is a great goal-scorer – one of the best of all time – but he is not close to Messi. Messi can score just as many goals and run games on his own and win them on his own too. Ronaldo can't do that to the same level.

I have to be honest and admit that I do understand those out there who believe Messi could be the greatest of all time. I never thought I would see anyone as good as Pele, but Messi comes close, for me. He is wonderful to watch. I would pay to watch him anytime. He could have played in any era of football. That is the biggest compliment I can give to him. He is extraordinary.

*****

John McGovern
Conquering Europe and character building with Cloughie

John McGovern was just sixteen when he made his professional debut in 1966 for Hartlepools, under the leadership of Brian Clough. Two years later Clough signed McGovern for Derby County where he won both the Second Division and First Division championships.

After a brief spell with Leeds United, McGovern once again linked up with Clough, this time at Nottingham Forest. McGovern was the captain of the side that won the First Division, two European Cups, two League Cups, one Charity Shield, and one European Super Cup.

You played at Derby County from 1968 to 1974 winning the First Division title in 1972 under Brian Clough. How would you sum up that period?

It was as impressive as what we went on to achieve at Forest in many ways. We won the Second Division championship in 1969 by seven points then within a few seasons, we win the First Division championship. That rise from the Second Division to becoming champions of England in three years was mostly down to Clough's burning ambition and Peter Taylor's remarkable recruitment.

The signing of Dave McKay was massive and that was down to Taylor. He was the talent scout as well as being assistant manager. Clough did recruit players too such as Colin Todd and John O'Hare. They were also great players who were brought in by Clough who had known them from Sunderland, but most of the recruitment was down to Taylor. As well as achieving domestic success at Derby, we also reached the semi-final of the European Cup which wasn't bad for the first attempt.

You joined Nottingham Forest under Brian Clough in 1974 however Peter Taylor was not with him initially. Did you notice a difference in Clough?

I did. I said to John O'Hare that it was as if Brian was going through the motions. There was not the same venomous verbals if a player did something that they shouldn't. Eventually, Peter joined Brian after a year then as a team we really took off. Again, the recruitment of players was very good, but they were also fortunate to have players like Ian Bowyer, Tony Woodcock, Martin O'Neill, Viv Anderson and John Robertson already at the club. Those five players went on to be international players, so they had the basis of a side. With that basis, they still had to get the best out of them, which Clough was an expert at doing.

We scraped promotion to the First Division on the last day of the season then we went on to sign Peter Shilton, Archie Gemmell and Kenny Burns. When you add that kind of quality to a young, hungry team and you've got the perfect formula.

We then go and sign the first £1,000,000 player in Trevor Francis and people ask if he was worth it? My response is that he scored the winner in the first European Cup final and that he repaid the £1,000,000 as soon as he scored that goal.

We then go on to achieve the miracle of retaining the European Cup at the first attempt.

Forest's European Cup success is widely considered to be one of the greatest achievements in football history. Would Clough change his approach for a European game at all?

No, he would never change. We didn't change the tactics much under Brian. He always put you in the right frame of mind so that when you went out on the pitch, you knew that you were expected to do your job and know your job. For example, in my early days of working with him, he would tell me 'I pay you to play midfield and if you can't play in midfield then I'll find someone else!

He wanted you to do what you were good at and try and improve the things that you weren't so good at. He didn't mind you making mistakes if you took responsibility for them and always tried to help the team.

I look back on my career and know that I lived the dream as a professional footballer. I loved every minute of it and I was very fortunate that Peter Taylor liked the look of me and told Brian Clough that I could play.

Finally John, what do you believe it was that made the Clough and Taylor partnership so successful?

My take on it is that you have two ambitious people that have different assets and are brilliant at what they do. If they were both brilliant instilling discipline and managing a side, then you would only need Clough. However, you need good players to build a successful team and Peter Taylor was brilliant at identifying players that were an ideal fit for the team.

Sometimes signings cost next to no money, so they were also able to build sides on a budget. They spent money at times too and broke transfer records on Trevor Francis and others, but there are also many examples of players like Dave McKay who they signed for next to nothing. They were both brilliant at different things so when they were united, it made them incredibly strong. The sad part of their story is that they then fell out after we won the European Cup for the second time. That partnership was never repaired, and I don't think they ever spoke again after that fallout.

*****

Andreas Brehme
Winning the World Cup

During a trophy laden career, Andreas Brehme represented Kaiserslautern, Bayern Munich, Inter Milan and Real Zaragoza, winning two Bundesligas, one German cup, one Serie A, one UEFA Cup and one World Cup, in which he scored the winning goal of the 1990 World Cup Final.

Scoring the winning goal in the 1990 World Cup final was iconic. Could you sum up that game against Argentina and what it was like to lift such a prestigious trophy?

The game was very intense and of course both teams knew each other very well. We were very confident we would win since we had grown as a team from the 1986 final. As a child I was dreaming, like many other children, about lifting the cup one day. So the moment I did a childhood dream came true! Our entire team had worked so hard to reach this goal.

Franz Beckenbauer was a great motivator and he managed to keep us on track for the ultimate win in 1990.

Playing a big tournament like the World Cup is not easy, especially when it comes to the knock-out phase. You need a high level of concentration every three days, but also need to be able to relax and unwind in between.

Ultimately the team spirit of the entire squad and backroom staff is most important. Including the preparation you are close together for more than six weeks, so the atmosphere within the team decides about the final success.

*****

Alan Mahood
When the final whistle blows... for good: The reality of retirement

Alan Mahood began his career in 1988 with Greenock Morton before moving to Nottingham Forest. After a season at the City Ground, Mahood rejoined Morton, making over one hundred appearances. Spells with Kilmarnock, Ross County and St Johnstone followed, before he signed for Morton for the third time. He retired in 2005 at the age of thirty-seven.

Some people are lucky enough to make the decision on their own, others less fortunate have it made for them. Then there's the guys in between who know it's time but can't let go due to the love of what they do or fear of what's to come.

When people in other walks of life talk about the 'R' word, it means leaving a job well into their sixties when they collect their pension, then think about much deserved time with grandchildren or a sun-soaked beach to while away the hours.

When you start out on your journey as a footballer you know it's a short-lived career, hoping to play for twenty years if you're lucky enough to avoid serious injury, but why worry about it? That's way ahead in the distance.

Then it seems like in the blink of an eye it's over: nobody wants you, no more going in to kick a ball about with your mates and getting paid for it.

So now what? Some will be fortunate enough to have made enough to give them a good lifestyle for the rest of their days. Some will have invested their money wisely in property or shares and be reaping the benefits. Some will even have spent their afternoons going back to education to improve their knowledge and chances of getting a job when they stop playing. Then there's the rest of us that went to the snooker hall after training, bite to eat then up the road before everybody else had even finished their nine-to-five dayshifts. Did we plan for the future? Nope!

We lived in our wee bubble thinking the day would never come. But it did. And with a BANG! Reality! What next? The real world.

Nobody to tell you what time to be somewhere and what colour t-shirt to wear that day. Nobody asking what you want to eat before telling you what's expected of you when you cross the white line. You're on your own. And even worse, must think for yourself. How do I survive? How do I get a job? Where do I even start? Fortunately, nowadays players are better informed helping them to be prepared to make the transition as smooth as possible, with mental health and personal well-being a big factor in this.

The big decision for every player is when do you call it a day? The easiest answer is your body will let you know, and with bells on! Your heart will think your legs can cover the ground, can go box to box, recover as quickly as you used to. Your head will tell you different. Your legs will ache after training, never mind the games. Young pups will be running past you the way you have done to older pros when you were coming through. It's starting to sink in. When you start to think about it, then you know it's around the corner. You will speak to loved ones, trusted allies, people you respect in football, looking for them to tell you to play for as long as you can, you'll regret chucking it too soon.

All kind words, but deep down, you know there's only one decision to make, the one you've been dreading since it first entered your mind. The one you know means the dream is over. But deep down you know your body better than anybody. Sometimes the hardest decisions are the easiest to make.

*****

Sammy McIllroy
From humble beginnings to the Theatre of Dreams

Sammy McIllroy joined Manchester United in 1969, becoming Sir Matt Busby's final signing. Over the next thirteen years he made over three hundred appearances for United, winning the Second Division championship, the FA Cup and the Charity Shield.

In 1982, McIllroy joined Stoke City for a club record fee of £350,000. He also played for Manchester City, Bury and Preston North End, before moving into management.

McIllroy earned eighty-five caps for Northern Ireland and played in two World Cups (1982 and 1986) and he also managed the nation between 2000 and 2003.

You were the last signing that Sir Matt Busby made for Manchester United in 1969. How proud are you of that fact so many years on?

I think more about it now than I did when I first found out about it, which is when I was still playing. Sir Matt Busby was a fantastic man and a fantastic manager who built Manchester United in many ways. The club would not have achieved the success that it did in subsequent decades after Sir Matt and be a worldwide club without his influence and impact. I am so proud to be his last signing of his even though I was only seventeen at the time and had a long way to go in the game.

Can you sum up what it is like when you swap life in Northern Ireland for Manchester to represent a club like United?

If I go back to my childhood, I wanted to be a footballer from my primary school days. George Best was coming through at that time and he was from the east side of Belfast. George was a superstar and someone that many in Northern Ireland looked up to. He was one of the main reasons that I wanted to be a footballer along with my father, who played amateur football himself in Belfast. My father was a great support for me and he did everything that he could to back me in my quest to become a footballer.

When you arrived at United, you were immediately training alongside some of the greatest players that the club has ever seen. How did you handle that level of pressure and expectation at a young age?

It was unbelievable. I walked into training on my first day and just to be around Charlton, Law, Best, Crerand, Stiles and all of the European greats was fantastic. There were times when I went home and I couldn't believe what I watched on the training field that day. I was just a young boy from Belfast who was used to watching these guys on my black and white television back home and here I was alongside them. Extraordinary.

I work regularly with Willie Morgan who always tells me that George was not the caricature that the media portrayed him as. There is also a saying – never meet your heroes. What was George like from your personal perspective?

Willie is spot on with his statement there. George was a very generous man who treated everyone with respect and dignity. I was only a kid, whereas Willie Morgan was an established teammate of his, but I can honestly say that he was great to be around. I was his teammate at Northern Ireland too and I only had fantastic times with him. He was a lovable character and it was the privilege of my life to share the same dressing room and pitch as him. It really was.

Can you talk me through your Manchester United debut, not everyone starts against Manchester City and scores on their debut too?

It was an incredible day. I honestly did not know that I was playing in that derby until the morning of the game. Frank O'Farrell was the manager at the time and Bill Foulkes was the reserve manager. Bill told me on the Friday evening that I was to report to Old Trafford at 11 am on the Saturday wearing a collar and tie.

I was actually a little disappointed to hear this news as normally the reserves of both sides meet at the same time as the two first teams and I wanted to play in that game. I honestly did not think I would be playing for the first team hence my disappointment. The morning of the game came around quickly and I got the bus from my digs to Warwick Road and walked into the ground. Not for a moment thinking about making my debut.

Frank was waiting for me at the front door and he told me that I would be taking Denis Law's place due to a failed fitness test. I was excited because I had no time to be nervous. George came over to me and said 'congratulations, Sammy, if you score today then I'll have a bottle of champagne for you on Monday morning.' To his credit, he sure did bring me a bottle of champagne in for me as I scored in a 3-3 draw with Manchester City. I have great memories from that day.

Every footballer has ups and downs in their career. You won trophies at United but also suffered relegation with the club. To younger generations of football fans, Manchester United being relegated seems impossible, but you experienced it for real. Just how would you put that period of your career into words?

Trust me, even back then no one thought that Manchester United could be relegated. It was only five years since we had won the European Cup. Unfortunately, that great side was breaking up and we went on a slide. I'll never forget the day that our fate was sealed against Manchester City.

It was a surreal feeling to think that the European champions of 1968 would be playing in the Second Division in 1974. It was mind-boggling and it took time to sink in. Tommy Docherty then rebuilt the club, and we were a very good side that dominated the second division to bounce straight back at the first attempt.

I have to be honest and say that the Second Division campaign was unbelievable. It was the most thrilling chapter of my career at Manchester United. The football we played was breathtaking and the fans backed us home and away with one hundred per cent faith that we would return at the first attempt.

Everyone in the side contributed. Gordan Hill and Steve Coppell were superb on the wings. Brian Greenhoff and Stuart Pearson were key as well. Martin Buchan and Jimmy Nicholl were solid at the back as well, and who could forget Lou Macari? He was excellent to play alongside.

The fans still talk about our team from the Second Division to this day which is special. We honestly had a relentless winning attitude that if the opposition scored two then we would score three or four. We always fancied our chances against any opposition.

You won the FA Cup with Manchester United in 1977 and were a runner up in 1976 and 1979. The FA Cup was a major focus of the English footballing calendar in that era. How proud were you to play in the cup final at Wembley on three occasions and get your hands on the trophy in '77?

For footballers of my era, they all wanted to play in the FA Cup final. It was the major showpiece occasion of that era with a full day of TV coverage from the BBC. It was every footballer's dream. The First Division and the European Cup were the pinnacles for a footballer in terms of success as they are today but back then the FA Cup was seen on an almost level footing as those trophies.

I was lucky to play in three finals even though we only won one of them. To beat Liverpool made it even sweeter in 1977. To stop them from winning the treble meant a lot because they were a formidable team at home and abroad in the '70s and '80s. Walking out at Wembley in front of a hundred thousand fans was literally a dream come true for me because I remember being the kid sitting in front of the television mesmerised at just watching those finals. To then go on and lift the trophy when the world is watching you is hard to put into words. It is absolutely brilliant and the highlight of anyone's life and career. I will never forget those memories.

You represented the club on four hundred and nineteen occasions. That is an incredible feat. How do you reflect on your time at Manchester United as a whole?

I was privileged to play for Manchester United on so many occasions and I was honestly heartbroken when I left the club under Ron Atkinson. I was only twenty-seven at the time and never wanted to leave the football club. I honestly believed that I had a lot of football left in me and that I could contribute to the club going forward.

Ron had other ideas for whatever reason and unfortunately, I had to leave the club. Looking back, I should have stayed and fought for my place. If I was given the opportunity to buckle down, I would have won my place back. Sadly, Atkinson did what he did and said what he said which dented my pride and I left hastily for Stoke City.

I loved every minute of my time representing Manchester United and I love going back to work at the club on a matchday now. It gives me great joy even today.

You played at Stoke City for three years and won the club's Player of the Year award. How did life in the Potteries differ from life in Manchester?

The fans loved me at Stoke which meant a lot. I got to play with Mickey Thomas again, too, which was nice because he was a terrific player. The team that I joined was a decent side with the likes of myself, Mickey, Paul Bracewell, Dave Watson, Steve Bould many others who had very good careers.

We were pushing to be a top ten First Division side, but it was not the same as United of course. It took time to adapt but I enjoyed my time at the club and the fans were always amazing towards me.

You represented your country on eighty-eight occasions, played at two World Cups and managed them as well. What did pulling on the Northern Ireland jersey and taking the reins of the national side mean to you and your family back home?

Those two World Cups were special. For a small nation of just over a million people just to get to the World Cup was an unbelievable achievement. We reached the knockouts, too, at Spain '82 which was even better. Unfortunately, Mexico '86 was tough for me personally and tinged with regret as my mother passed away while I was playing in the tournament. That is still a wrench for me.

From 1980 to 1986, we had a special team who won the Home Nations tournament and reached two World Cups. Those were great days for Northern Irish football.

I have to ask you about Norman Whiteside. When I interviewed him previously, he spoke highly of how you looked after him as a young up and coming player. Did he remind you or yourself coming through as a youngster?

We are best pals. We played snooker every Wednesday for years in Manchester. Unfortunately, Norman found out that he had a neck injury and could no longer play which was a shame. As a seventeen-year-old kid coming through, I could see right away that he was going to be a top player.

The sad thing is that he never fulfilled his potential due to injury which is a great shame. He would have been one of the all-time greats of Manchester United if it were not for his injury. I still work with him now at the club on a matchday and on *MUTV*. It is always great to catch up with him.

As a manager, you had success with Macclesfield and Morecambe. How did management compare to playing the game?

We won everything that we could realistically win at Macclesfield which was great. We were a success which led to me getting the Northern Ireland job. The chairman at the time, Malcolm Jones, backed me to the hilt and we got our rewards from that. Following my time with Northern Ireland, Morecambe came along and I got them out of the Conference and into the Football League as well. We got to the play-offs twice and could have reached League One which would have been unbelievable at that time. It is where the club is today which is good to see.

Management was very good but let me tell you something from the heart, I've been in football since the age of fourteen. I am now sixty-seven and I can honestly tell you nothing beats playing the game.

Playing is the best thing that you can do in the game. Don't get me wrong, when things are going well, management is great but that can change in a matter of months. Playing is the dream.

No doubt about that. I still try and play today because I love the game of football as much as I always have.

*****

Shaun Maloney
From the training pitch to Paradise (and back!)

Shaun Maloney joined Celtic in 1999 and made his debut two years later in the Old Firm match. Over the next six years, Maloney won five Scottish Premier Leagues, three League Cups and was runner up in the 2003 UEFA Cup.

After leaving Celtic Park, Maloney won the FA Cup with Wigan in 2013. He also played for Aston Villa, Chicago Fire and Hull City.

Shaun moved into management in 2021; first with Hibs and then with Wigan.

You came into the Celtic first team in the era of Henrik Larsson and Martin O'Neill in the early 2000s. How did it feel to train with those players and then play alongside them?

Believe it or not, I actually did not train with them regularly before I made my debut against Rangers in 2001. I trained only once before making my debut and that was the day before the match itself.

I was taken out of a reserve game at half-time and told that I would be training with the first team the following day. I had only played for the reserve team twice prior to that so everything moved quickly for me at Celtic at that time.

I had trained twice with the first team prior to Martin O'Neill arriving at the club but that was down to luck on my part because two youth players would be ball boys at first-team training. On two occasions when I was doing that under John Barnes due to an injury in a training match, I was asked to fill in. Those were the first opportunities that I had to train with the first team, but I was just an extra body, so it was not until the day before my debut that I trained with them on merit.

Only training with them once before playing meant that I did not have a massive build-up to match day and meant that I was not too fazed by who I was playing with or against.

Can you talk me through what your debut was like given such little build-up in training?

Well, it was between myself and Mark Fotheringham as to which young player would be on the bench for the game against Rangers. We were roommates in a house in Barrhead but thankfully, on the day, it was me who made the squad for the game. Despite that, Mark and I still had to put the kit and the boots out pre-match because we were a part of the ground staff, like all YTS players.

Then, the match itself did not feel too alien to me because I had travelled with the first team as part of the ground staff before, so I had experienced that environment before. Even when I came on, due to my age and inexperience at the time, I did not fully understand the magnitude of everything that is associated with playing in games against Rangers or how special beating them 3-0 was.

You quickly establish yourself in the Celtic first team under Martin O'Neill and you played in the run to the UEFA Cup Final of 2003. What was Martin like as a manager for a young player like yourself?

First and foremost, Martin had played the game to such a high level and as a two-time European Cup winner, he commanded respect from everyone in the dressing room. As a manager, he was hard but fair. His instructions were clear, and his demands were obvious to everyone within the team. If you performed well then you would earn the right to stay in his team and if you did not, then you knew that you were out.

He had such an aura as a person, and I have never experienced another manager or coach with that aura since. The environment he created at Celtic was ultra competitive. Every training session was life or death. You had to be at the top of your game every single day because the demand to win was always there. It did not matter if it was a training session, a friendly, or a competitive game. You had to win.

As a forward player, how much did you learn from Henrik Larsson, Chris Sutton and John Hartson in particular?

Henrik was of such a high standard that he was a level above everyone else at the club. He was genuinely one of the best forward players in the European game during his time at Celtic. He still had time for younger players and was gracious with his time. He was great with me with advice in training when it came to making runs for example.

Chris and John were similar too. They were both very good and wanted to create a partnership with you that would help the team on a match day.

Outside those three, Paul Lambert was also an amazing player in his position and someone who I learned a lot from. He could talk you through a game and was also a European cup winner, like Martin O'Neill.

Tom Boyd was similar at the beginning of my career. He was the perfect captain.

Steve Guppy also had a big influence on my career. I ended up rooming with him and Steve was great with me. He set a positive example to younger players because he got absolutely everything out of his career through hard work and dedication. He would spend time with me after training to work on my technical skills.

Looking back, I was very fortunate to have many top players and characters to learn from in a sink-or-swim environment.

You picked up a serious injury in Martin O'Neill's last season in charge. Every player wants to impress the next manager so did it worry you that Gordon Strachan replaced Martin while you were still working on returning from injury?

It had a big impact on me, for sure. I had a full off-season where I knew that I had to work extra hard to regain match sharpness and overall fitness to impress Gordon Strachan when he arrived at the club.

I was actually on the verge of leaving the club on loan when Gordon arrived due to the lack of games that I had played in the previous season because of my knee injury. I had interest from two SPFL clubs and one English Championship side but, thankfully, I was able to force myself into Gordon's plans in pre-season and stay at the club.

Eventually, I earned my place in the team and never looked

back during that season. I thrived by playing regularly rather than coming on partway through a game for Larsson, Sutton, Hartson or Bellamy, who were all top strikers who were at the club when Martin was in charge.

Remarkably, you won the PFA Player of the Year and PFA Young Player of the Year in that very season. Your form led to interest in you from several clubs and you linked up with Martin O'Neill again at Aston Villa in January 2007. Was Martin the big factor in getting you to Villa?

Yeah, he was, but I never wanted to leave Celtic. Even up until deadline day when I left for Villa, I still wanted to stay at Celtic. I wanted to sign a long-term contract with the club, but it became apparent that both sides were not going to meet, and I left for Villa.

I was young at the time, but I regret not being more hands-on during that time because if I had the chance to sit down with Gordon and the owner of the club then I do not think I would ever have left. I wanted to stay and the club wanted me to stay but once an agreement was not reached, Villa bid and I joined up with Martin again.

Villa is a massive club who have won the European Cup in their history. I was fortunate that I was joining another big club under a manager who I knew had faith in me. I enjoyed my time at Aston Villa as a whole and playing in the Premier League was a great experience too.

Physically, it was more demanding than playing in Scotland due to the speed of the game and the amount of running that you had to do within a game. That was partly due to us facing teams such as Manchester United and co who dominated possession whereas, at Celtic, we dominated possession in every domestic game that we played.

Playing against teams like the Manchester United team that won the Champions League in 2008 was great. They had players such as Rooney, Ronaldo, Tevez, Giggs, Scholes, Ferdinand and Vidic.

The level of opposition was high every single week and I thoroughly enjoyed my time at Aston Villa. I am so glad that I experienced Villa at that time because we finished sixth in one of the best leagues in world football.

You returned to Celtic in 2008 after eighteen months at Villa Park. How did your second spell at Celtic compare with your first spell at the club?

I wanted to return to Celtic at the first available opportunity because all I ever wanted to do as a young boy was play for Celtic. I grew up as a Celtic fan and, as I said earlier, I never wanted to leave the club when I did in my first spell. I loved the pressure that comes with being a Celtic player. I love the history and heritage that the club has and I missed that when I was away. Playing for *your* team is like no other feeling in football. I missed that and wanted it back.

Overall, my second spell was one of transition. I also really struggled with injury, which did not help matters. I was injury free when I returned for the first six months then I did not have regular spells where I was able to play more than fifteen games without another injury.

Unfortunately, the injuries I suffered were serious and I was not able to become a big part of the team which was difficult because that is not how I wanted things to go especially at the club that I love. We also had great moments where we took the league to the last day in 2009 and won the League Cup in that season. We should have won that league.

Then, Gordon leaves and Tony Mowbray comes in. I loved Tony and, for me, he was the right manager at the right club but at the wrong time. It was a period of real transition and, unfortunately, Tony loses his job less than a season after taking over, then Neil Lennon comes in as interim manager then as permanent manager.

Neil had some great moments as Celtic manager and I have so much time for Neil. However, I knew that it was the end of the cycle for many of our players when Neil came in and you have to accept that and move on.

Although my second spell was tough at the time, I do not regret coming back to Celtic because I was at the place where I most wanted to play football.

You joined Wigan Athletic from Celtic and worked with Roberto Martinez for the first time. You scored some memorable goals, particularly against Manchester United, to save the club from relegation and you won the FA Cup in 2013. Can you sum up what your time at Wigan was like as a whole?

Roberto was brilliant to work for. The way that he set the team up and trusted us to play good football made us believe that on our day, we could beat anybody.

In terms of the Manchester United goal, I am actually a Manchester United fan! They were the English club that I followed growing up and, being from Aberdeen, Sir Alex Ferguson was like a God to us. I would travel down to watch United at Old Trafford as a kid from school with the family but the goal that I scored against them was one of my most important because it kept us in the league that season.

We needed to win or we were in big trouble, but it was an incredible night. We were very good throughout the game and we deserved our victory. It was a performance that epitomised our approach under Roberto Martinez.

It was not a realistic ambition for us to think that we could win a major trophy in England such as the FA Cup given our budget compared the rest of the teams in the Premier League. However, that is what we achieved and it was the stuff of fairytales. We beat a top-class Manchester City team managed by Roberto Mancini at Wembley, which is such an iconic ground. It was the perfect day in many ways.

Ben Watson's header to win the game is one of the best headers that I have ever seen. If you watch the goal back, the angle at which he connects with the ball and where it hits the back of the net is extraordinary. It reminded me of the goal that Cristiano Ronaldo scored against Roma in the Champions League for Manchester United a few years prior.

The best thing about winning that day was the fact that we went toe to toe with Manchester City. We created chances, we had similar possession and we deserved to win the game. They had players such as Yaya Toure, David Silva, Sergio Aguero and Vincent Kompany which makes it all the more pleasing when I look back because they were world-class.

Lifting the cup was a moment of pure joy. My family were at Wembley and that moment was the happiest that I have ever felt on a football pitch. No one expected us to win that trophy, but we did it and it brought memories back of watching the FA Cup on TV as a kid with my dad. To be a part of the history of the FA Cup when you think of some of the iconic moments that have come before in the competition, like Gascoigne's free kick or Cantona's volley, is magical.

You represented Scotland on forty-seven occasions and scored seven goals. What are your personal highlights from your time with the national team?

It was a huge privilege to play for my country whenever I had the opportunity to do so. I have done every role as an international player. I've travelled and not played; I've come off the bench in games and I've started in key games too. It was such a huge source of pride for me and every cap meant the world to me. I love living in Scotland and I'll always call Scotland home, so to be able to pull on that jersey was something that felt amazing every time.

Following your retirement from playing, you moved into coaching with Celtic then the Belgian national team. What did you learn from those coaching roles in particular?

I learned so much from working at Celtic under-20s when Brendan Rodgers was manager. That gave me a good grounding before Roberto called me and asked me to join him at Belgium. I learned so much from working with him because at Belgium, he was working with world-class players and as such, the tactical side of the game was incredibly detailed, and the demands were very high because of the standard of player he had.

Working with elite players was great for me as a young coach too because they are engaging and trust you to help them find new ways to beat opponents. Creating connections with them was important as was developing my sessions to tailor them to what the team needed. It was a massive privilege for me to work with Roberto and I loved working with young players as well as with experienced players like Kompany, Alderweireld and Vermaelen because you learned from them too.

CHAPTER TWO
Management

Roy Hodgson
Managing across the world

Roy Hodgson began his managerial career almost forty years ago. During that time, Hodgson has won several trophies, including the Swedish league title and the Danish league title, and has finished runner up in the UEFA Cup and Europa League.

Hodgson's career has taken him all over the world with notable spells at Malmö, Copenhagen, Inter Milan, Liverpool, Fulham, West Brom, Crystal Palace and Watford. He has also managed on the international stage with Switzerland, England, Finland and the United Arab Emirates.

During your career in football – which we will come to shortly – you have learned to speak five different languages. Have you always had a passion for languages and culture from a young age?

I would not call it a passion but at school, I was much more on the arts side than the science side. I studied French and Latin at school which we were obliged to study in those days. I did not have any real mastery of French until I lived in Switzerland if the truth be told because we were not taught in a conversational style.

The other languages that I have learned have been through necessity because I needed them to be able to communicate properly in the countries that I worked in. I learned each language in different ways. Italian was the most difficult for me because I never had any formal lessons. I learned Italian by listening as I went along and it is by far and away the worst grammatically that I speak as a result.

The languages in which I am truly fluent are English, French and Swedish. With the others, I can converse in terms that are linked to football rather go too far outside of that.

You have had great success managing in Scandinavian football at club level in Sweden, Denmark and Norway. You won titles with two different clubs in Sweden and with FC Copenhagen in Denmark. What inspired you to move to Scandinavia and how do you reflect on your spells with Halmstads BK and Malmö in particular?

What got me to Sweden was the offer of a job when I was really young at Halmstads BK in 1976. I had played football in South Africa then had just returned home to the UK and was playing in non-league football while also coaching PE at a school in London.

Then, suddenly this offer came in from Halmstads BK. It was tough to give up what I was doing but I also wanted to grasp the opportunity to become a full-time coach in the top division of Swedish football.

The club had narrowly survived relegation the year before I arrived. It could have been seen as a hopeless task and I believe that many other Swedish managers turned the job down because they did not think that the job was doable. I went in more naively at that stage of my career because I was happy to be offered such an opportunity.

What happened after that meant a lot to me as we won two titles in five years, the first title was one in our first season which was a Cinderella story in Sweden. Akin to Leicester winning the Premier League if you like. Of course, I am not suggesting that it was the same level of achievement as Swedish football is not the Premier League but in terms of how that title win was looked upon, it was similar.

I had jobs at Bristol City, and Orebro SK back in Sweden after moving on from Halmstads BK before taking the Malmö job in 1985. My time at Malmö was a wonderful time as we won five league titles in a row and win the cup twice.

It was a golden period and led to me going to manage in

Switzerland and then Italy. Malmö was the catalyst for launching my career to a more well-known level, so I owe both Halmstads BK and Malmö an awful lot for the success that I had over in Sweden.

You have managed one of the biggest clubs in European football history at Internazionale on two occasions. What was it like to manage in Serie A during a time of real quality in Italian football?

Inter Milan was my first opportunity and experience of managing a club where the spotlight is on you every single minute of the day and night. Even pre-season friendlies are scrutinised with enormous interest. I had never really had that before in my career although I did have a lot of experience coaching and managing players.

The political side — mass media and the pressure from anyone who appears to be near the club — was new to me at that time and it was an important experience to get given how the rest of my career would pan out.

I was lucky that the chairman of the club, Massimo Moratti — and Giacinto Facchetti who was his right-hand man — really took me under their wings and supported me. The players were also good because they took to the work that we were doing and helped me through my time at the club.

What was it like to walk out into the San Siro as Inter Milan manager at each home game?

Unfortunately, I fear that when you are in a job, a lot of those wonderful experiences which should be indelibly printed on your memory such as walking out at San Siro are not there because you solely focused on the game ahead, the tactics that you have employed and the opposition that you are facing.

It is a privilege to be in that position but in the heat of the moment, you do not really take in those wonderful moments. It is only now upon reflection that you start to realise what momentous occasions they were.

You have extensive experience managing at international level with Switzerland, the UAE, Finland and England. How does international football compare with managing at club level?

Apart from the actual coaching, which is the same as it is at club level, albeit with a shorter timeframe due to the international breaks that are spread out across a season, it is very different.

You actually have more choice of who you want to work with because at club level, you walk into a club and you inherit between twenty-five and thirty-five players. All of whom are under contract, which you cannot do much about. You can try and move players on that are not going to be in your plans to generate money to reinvest in recruiting your own players but that can be easier said than done.

At international level, you also do not have to deal with agents to any great extent and you are able to invite the players to the national team that you believe are the right players for you which is not the case at club level.

The actual job is the same in terms of working with the players and your staff to win football matches albeit without being able to build the same sort of bond that you can at club level due to the time constraints of the international breaks. As a result, the job becomes somewhat more ambassadorial because you are representing the nation you are in charge of as a footballing nation in many different capacities.

You become a figurehead for the nation's football, which is not the case at club level because no matter how big the club that you are managing is, within the country that you are in there are other high-profile clubs.

The nature of the fans is also different at international level. At a match for one of the Manchester clubs or Merseyside clubs, the fans at the game will still mostly be Mancunian or Liverpudlian. Whereas at international level, the fans in the stadium may be majority local to a given area where the game is but the result impacts fans across the full nation.

Staying on the theme of international football, how did managing your native England compare with managing other nations? Does extra emotional investment come into play at all or did you approach the role as you normally would?

I tried to approach the England job in a way that I normally would but, of course, it is the greatest honour to be invited to manage the nation's football team of your native country. I was very much aware of that. I was also aware of this honour when I was in Switzerland and Finland but not being Swiss or Finnish, I would admit that I felt it more when I was managing England.

That being said, I still invested all of my time to succeeding with Switzerland and Finland just as a Swiss or Finnish manager would have done for his country.

One can't deny that being offered the job of managing your native country is a different feeling because you grow up dreaming of playing for England which I was not able to do as a player. So, when the opportunity arises as a manager, it is an important moment in your life as a whole, not just your footballing life.

One of your most memorable jobs in football management was at Fulham whom you led from fighting a relegation battle to the Europa League final in just two and a half seasons. What were the key factors to that turnaround and how proud are you of what you achieved at Fulham?

It was a very big achievement. There is no doubt about that. It was down to a management structure that supported me. I worked with two CEOs in David McNally and Alastair McIntosh with whom I had great relationships.

Mohamed Al Fayed was the owner of the club and he put a lot of responsibility on both CEOs to run the club financially and in an administrative sense. That support then filtered down to me and my suggestions were taken on. Fulham was probably the only club that I managed in England — to some extent, also West Bromwich Albion — where I was able to recruit players that I wanted to work with and who I thought would make the team better.

My time at Crystal Palace was also excellent and the support there was very good too but there was not a lot of money to buy players. What we were able to do was ok and I was very much involved in the recruitment process despite us not being able to afford players that could make a vast difference. Thankfully, that changed under Patrick Vieira. Palace have been able to recruit players to improve the squad and increase the chances of success.

You have managed many world-class footballers such as Ronaldo

Nazario, Javier Zanetti, Steven Gerrard and Roberto Baggio to name just a few. What is it like as a coach when you are working at great teams with world-renowned individuals like those? Do you have to manage them in a particular way at all?

Looking back, I should have treated them in a different way than I did. I only worked with Baggio and Ronaldo for a short time in my second spell at Inter. Around three and half months. It was at the end of Baggio's career when the club was in a little bit of turmoil.

Unfortunately, Ronaldo was injured while I was at Inter. Of course, I could claim that I worked with the great Ronaldo, but we did not have the chance to work together often due to the new injury that he suffered at the time which subsequently ended his career in years to come.

When working with top players, one should do them the service of recognising that their talents are greater than others within the team. Of course, you still treat everyone fairly and with respect equally, but you cannot suggest that every player is of equal importance within a football team because we know that if you lose one or two key individuals that it can make a massive difference.

A team that is challenging for a title can easily fall closer to mid-table if they lose two of their key players. Fellow players also recognise that. They know that everyone has to be treated fairly but that there are different levels of leeway granted to players because you have to make sure that your top players are happy and want to be at your club. Otherwise, everyone loses if they leave and your team becomes a weaker group.

Respect has to be shared equally and professionalism has to be shown by all equally too. Although, you do sometimes need to be more tolerant of behaviour at certain times from your star players because your intolerance can create unnecessary conflict.

You do not want to create a conversation of who is more important: the star player or the manager, because anyone that has worked in football at a high level knows that football players win football matches. They are the most important pieces in the chess set that is the football club.

Last but not least, Roy, given your extensive experience as a manager and head coach, I have to ask you about working with a strong backroom staff. How important is it to strike a balance between leading by example as head coach and being able to delegate to your staff? Did your approach to this evolve over the course of your career or remain relatively similar?

My approach has evolved over the years.

At Halmstads BK, which was my first club, I did not have a staff. I was then given an assistant manager who was appointed by the club. He was from the sports platoon of the local army barracks and although he was a wonderful help and foil for me, he was not hired for his footballing knowledge because football was not his first sport, nor did he have any footballing qualifications.

I rarely had the luxury of building a staff that I wanted until relatively late at Fulham. For example, I inherited staff at Blackburn who I had a strong working relationship with and who were great. I was fortunate that the staff at many of the clubs that I worked at were very good and that I inherited them when I got there.

When it comes to delegation, I paid more attention to it as my career progressed. I realise that I should have delegated much more even at Fulham. I would recommend to any manager who is putting their own staff together to delegate especially if you are selecting coaches with particular strengths and talents. It is imperative that they are given the room to showcase those talents and that is something that I have been able to do much better in recent years.

However, as I say, I have not always been able to choose a staff that I particularly want. It has been more of a case of me going into a job that I want to do and inheriting staff whom I then build relationships with in order to allow them to jump on board with me. That has been the case for the bulk of my career.

*****

Brian McDermott
From chief scout to Premier League manager

Brian McDermott began his career at Arsenal in 1979. During his time at Highbury, he spent loan spells at Fulham and IFK Norrköping in Sweden, before joining Oxford United in 1984.

Before he retired in 1995, McDermott also played for

Huddersfield Town, <u>Djurgårdens IF</u>, Cardiff City, Exeter and Yeovil.

McDermott then moved into management and took Reading to the Premier League in 2012. He managed Leeds United in 2013, before returning to Reading two years later.

You started your playing career at Arsenal as an apprentice in the late 1970s. What was it like for you to be in at Arsenal during that era?

I started at QPR and was let go. Then I was at Millwall on trial and they didn't take me. I then had a similar trial at Arsenal and managed to scrape in as an apprentice. Seven people at the club were tasked with making the decision about signing me; four of them wanted me to sign and three didn't. That is how close it was.

After that, thankfully I did okay and I signed a professional contract with Arsenal at the age of seventeen and made my first team debut at the same age in February 1979, against Bristol City. I was based in Slough and I did not want to move into digs because I was happy at home so each day was long with the travelling in and from training each day for me.

I have to say that Arsenal are a top club with great values. I feel very fortunate and proud to have played for and worked for Arsenal off the field too.

How do you reflect back on your playing career at Arsenal as a whole?

I did not break into the team and play regularly like Paul Davis, for example, did. I played around seventy games for Arsenal and scored thirteen goals within that time without ever being a first pick. I should have left earlier to get more first-team opportunities elsewhere, in all honesty.

I had a few loan spells away from Arsenal during that time too as I was never able to fully crack it at Arsenal by becoming a consistent figure in the team. I was a bit-part player over the piece, really, which is nothing to be ashamed of.

One of the loan spells that you had away from Arsenal was to

IFK Norrköping in Swedish football. What was your experience of playing abroad at a young age like?

When I went to Sweden I was the main player in the team, and, to be honest, I needed that. I flourished during my time with IFK Norrköping and ended up winning Player of the Year, which was nice. I scored five goals in seventeen games and was playing with confidence. They wanted me to stay and I also had a few offers from other Swedish clubs which I should probably have taken in hindsight. I thoroughly enjoyed my time in Sweden, however, my priority was to return to England because that is what I knew best.

Upon returning to England, you went on to represent clubs such as Oxford United, Cardiff City, Exeter and Yeovil before you entered the world of coaching. Was a career in coaching on your mind during your playing career?

Not really, it just kind of happened that way. I got my first coaching badge at twenty-eight because I thought I should get one just in case, but it was never part of a masterplan that I had.

I ended up at Slough Town when I stopped playing and set up their football in the community programme. For two years I coached kids, and girls' football was part of that too which was unique in the 1990s. We had a great uptake in that back then, so it is wonderful to see how popular women's football is now across the globe. I really enjoyed my role doing that until the opportunity to become the first team manager of Slough Town arose and I decided to take the opportunity.

You managed Slough Town and Woking in non-league football before joining Reading initially as a scout and youth team coach. How much did you enjoy those roles?

I really enjoyed working with Alan Pardew at the club before he left for West Ham United. Then, Steve Coppell came in and did a fantastic job at the club. He was great for me because he had belief in me and what I could offer.

On his first day at the club, he brought me into his office and said, 'I want you to stay with us and I want you to find me players. It was as simple as that and that is what I strived to do. It was my dream job to be working on the recruitment side because I love the challenge of watching and finding players.

I was also coaching the reserves at that time too. I worked with Nigel Gibbs who did most of the training to allow me to carry out my role as chief scout, which took me all over the world, but on a match day, I took the team. That kept my hand in on the coaching and managerial front.

Steve is a great guy and I worked with Nick Hammond who was previously director of football at Celtic too. We won the Championship in 2006 with a record 106 points to reach the Premier League, which is remarkable considering we worked in the black and did not overspend or go into debt.

The likes of Dave Kitson, Leroy Lita, Kevin Doyle, Shane Long, Steve Sidwell and others were brought in, all who went on to be top players for Reading and also have good careers overall. Reading were a great club with fabulous people.

Brendan Rodgers replaced Steve Coppell and things did not work out which led to you taking caretaker charge. Did you approach the role on a game-by-game basis or were you planning for the longer term?

Brendan Rodgers is a top coach who has managed some of the biggest clubs in the UK with Liverpool and Celtic. However, he left and I was asked to take the team which I did.

I always approached my managerial career on a game-by-game basis and when I was asked to step in, I was not looking for the job full-time. I knew all of the players as I had signed most of them so when I stepped up to manage the team, Nick Hammond continued to work hard on the recruitment side.

Nigel Gibbs came in as my assistant and because I knew all of the staff at the club, it was a good fit. That being said, in my first three games, we drew two and got smashed by Plymouth. Then, the next game was Liverpool in the FA Cup which after two points from a possible nine was a daunting prospect. However, we drew 1-1 with Liverpool at home and then beat them in the replay at Anfield.

I was offered the job after that, but it was not officially announced until a few weeks later. Thankfully, we went on a good run in the league after a shaky start that saw me take two points from fifteen, albeit with FA Cup wins over Liverpool and Burnley, who were both Premier League sides, in between. We reached the quarter-final of the cup that season which was a good achievement given where we were in the Championship at the time.

You led Reading to the Play-Off final at Wembley in 2011 where the club lost out to Swansea and former manager Brendan Rodgers. Despite that disappointment, you rallied the players to go on and win the Championship title in 2012. Looking back, what was the key to that turnaround?

Funnily enough, I do a presentation on that season for the LMA now called: Losing, Winning, Mental Health and Finding Balance.

It took great resilience to bounce back after losing a game as high profile as the Play-Off final. It was a poignant time for me as the manager of Reading because I honestly thought that we had blown our chance of returning to the Premier League. I could not let anyone else know that I was thinking that way or that I was struggling personally. So, we went through a kind of mourning period at the start of the next season by losing five of the first seven games.

In this current era, you would be sacked for that sort of form at the start of a season, but I think patience was shown because I had taken the team to the final only a matter of months previously. We turned it around and the rest is history because we became a Premier League team again. It was a momentous journey that took a lot out of everyone at the club.

What did it feel like to manage in the Premier League having started your managerial career in non-league football?

It was surreal, but the journey is possible. It happened for me and sometimes you need luck to be on your side. I was in the right place at the right time and with great staff and players around me, we had success at Reading. It is never easy to put that together, but we did and we were a Premier League team again.

The ownership of the club then changed during that time when Anton Zingarevich bought the club. Unfortunately, we did not have the finances that we thought we would have and I went from winning Premier League Manager of the Month in January 2013 to being sacked six weeks later in March 2013. That sums up the madness of football and what can sometimes can happen.

Looking back, I am proud to have had the privilege of managing in the Premier League as not many people have the opportunity to do that in their careers.

Your next job after Reading was Leeds United. Were you nervous about taking the job given the rate of managerial change that Leeds had at that time?

It was not that, but I wanted to take over when the season had ended but due to the club's form, I was asked to take over early in April to help the club avoid relegation. We won the first two games which secured our Championship status which was nice.

I knew the history of Leeds when I went there. It is a juggernaut of a club. The fans are incredible and the atmosphere at Elland Road was always unbelievably strong. We started my first full season in charge by beating Brighton and at Christmas, we were in amongst the play-off teams.

Then a change of ownership happened and the next three months were carnage at the club. I was sacked on 31 January on transfer deadline day, before reinstating me two days later. I could write a book on that time. Then, at the end of May, I went for good, but I knew it was only a matter of time after the madness of late January.

Despite that, I still have a lot of time for Leeds United and the fans. They gave me and the team their backing home and away. What [Marcelo] Bielsa did to take them back to the Premier League was incredible, and good luck to them.

You returned to Arsenal after your time in charge at Leeds to work with Arsene Wenger. How did it feel to return to the club where you started your career?

It was amazing. I worked under Steve Rowley who was the chief scout at the time and also Francis Cagiago who is now working at the Chilean FA. I had a wonderful time there, albeit a short time, as Reading came calling again, but it is a wonderful club.

Finally, Brian, you left your second spell as Reading manager in 2017. Do you see yourself returning to management again or has that ship sailed as far as you are concerned?

I went back to Reading for a second spell then returned to Arsenal again after that. During Covid, I left Arsenal due to staffing cuts and now I am doing my presentation to corporate clients and football clubs too.

I believe that is important to highlight the mental health side of football and that is something that I am looking to do by speaking openly in my presentation about the reality of top-level management. I am also working on a mentoring programme with the LMA. I am doing plenty of stuff and I enjoy working. I want to do the best that I possibly can and I love football.

*****

Martin O'Neill
Success and man management

Martin O'Neill signed for Nottingham Forest in 1971 and during his decade at the City Ground, he won the First Division, the League Cup and two European Cups. After leaving Forest in 1981, he played for Norwich, Manchester City and Notts County before moving into management with non-league Grantham Town.

Following a successful spell at Wycombe, O'Neill took over at Norwich City before joining Leicester City in 1996 where he led the club to promotion to the Premier League in his first season. He followed that up with two League Cup victories, before taking over at Celtic in 2000.

During his five years at Celtic, O'Neill won three league titles, three Scottish Cups, one Scottish League Cup and finished runners up in the 2003 UEFA Cup.

O'Neill has also managed Aston Villa, Sunderland, Republic of Ireland and Nottingham Forest.

I want to start by asking you about Brian Clough and Nottingham Forest. How quickly was Clough able to transform the club following his arrival in 1975?

Brian Clough absolutely transformed the club from top to bottom throughout his time in charge at Nottingham Forest. However, it was the arrival of Peter Taylor to work alongside Brian which is when we saw the very best of Clough.

He took us from being a struggling Second Division side — the league that you would now call the Championship — who did not seem to be progressing too far, to becoming champions of England and back-to-back champions of European football. It is hard to imagine that ever happening again in the same manner in the modern game.

Although Brian was instantly charismatic success did not follow immediately upon his arrival. It was around eighteen months after his arrival when Taylor arrived as his assistant that we really started to take off even though he had gradually put his imprint on the side.

You won the First Division title and the League Cup in 1979. That success is followed with back-to-back European Cup victories in 1979 and 1980 with a Super Cup victory in between. Can you put your finger on exactly what it was that Clough and Taylor were able to do that made Forest immortal in footballing terms?

The key to their approach was that it was remarkably simple. Not for one minute did Brian Clough not know about tactics because, of course, he did, however, he did not pay too much attention to the opposition. Everything was tailored around what we could do to hurt the opposition rather than worrying about their perceived strengths.

Brian would not be dismissive of talented players or teams, but he seldom spoke about them in the lead-up to a game. He was always very positive and he kept his messages to us as players clear and concise. He never over-complicated us as players with umpteen messages before a game which I agree with because no matter how smart you are as a player, you do not want a dozen instructions to worry about before a game. If there are too many instructions from a manager then you start to wonder who should be taking to the field. Everyone knew their job in his side and it was a matter of doing it to the best of your ability which we often did.

How did playing on the European stage with Forest compare with playing in the English top flight?

That's a good question. Brian Clough did not alter his approach from domestic football to European competition. The only difference that we would sometimes encounter would be a sense of going into the unknown against certain opponents because we did not have the instant access to information on players from all leagues and clubs like we do now thanks to Google and the likes.

For example, our quarter-final opponents in the second European Cup success were Dynamo Berlin. While we knew that they were a fine side, we relied on first-hand accounts from scouting as to what they were like as opposed to being able to sit and watch clips of them in action. That was the only major difference between both competitions.

The trophies that Forest won under Clough speak for themselves and the legacy of that team will live forever. Given you played a big part in that, what were your personal highlights from that era at the club?

My personal highlight is winning the second European Cup because I was on the field of play in that game, as opposed to the first success when I was injured. Being on the field when the final whistle is blown to crown your team champions of European is incredibly special. That is a terrific memory.

Another memory that sticks out is the semi-final against Cologne at the City Ground which was the most atmospheric I have ever heard the stadium. We drew 3-3 on the night which meant that we had to go away and win in Germany to get to the final. Thankfully, we were able to do that and reach the final to cap off a wonderful run in the competition.

As well as representing Forest, you played for clubs such as Manchester City and Norwich City. However, I want to focus on your international career with Northern Ireland because you captained your country at the World Cup in 1982. How much does that mean to you when you look back?

It was another incredible moment for me in my career but also an incredible moment for the country. For us to beat the host nation Spain and qualify for the quarter-finals of a World Cup was nothing short of remarkable. What made that victory even more special for us was such a tough game as Mal Donaghy was sent off and we had to hang on against Spain. It was terrific and that game is like yesterday to me because it meant so much to everyone at the time.

You went into football management following your retirement as a player. Was that always the plan post-retirement?

Absolutely not (laughs). Believe it or not, it was not on my mind at all despite the fact that I worked under Clough and Taylor who were two of the best teachers you could ask for.

I did not think about it until I met Peter Taylor in Nottingham city centre a couple of years after retiring. He told me that he thought I would go on to become a manager which surprised me. He told me that he was disappointed that I did not go into management after retiring which led to me giving it much thought when I went home that evening. That chat resonated with me and I started to apply for managerial posts that were vacant at the time.

The managerial post that put you on the map was at Wycombe Wanderers who you led into the Football League from the conference with a haul of trophies along the way. How do you reflect on your time at the club overall?

Wycombe was a terrific time in my career and a vitally important time in my career too because if I had failed at Wycombe then the chances are that I would not have had another managerial opportunity in football. Thankfully, things worked out positively for myself and for the club and I can honestly say that I put my heart and soul into Wycombe during my time in charge.

You left Wycombe for Norwich City before moving on to Leicester City. You win promotion to the Premier League at Leicester and follow that success up with two League Cup victories at Wembley. What are your standout memories from that time in your career?

We had a really poor start at Leicester when I arrived. The fans were in uproar because it seemed like I could not win a game. Things were a real struggle. I think it took me eight league games to register my first wins which made me think even at that early stage that any chance of promotion was gone. However, credit to the players and my staff, we battled back and took off from there which led to us winning promotion to the Premier League which was the aim.

I absolutely loved my time at Leicester and winning the League Cups was special and a great moment for the players and fans alike. Hopefully, they still remember it fondly if they can excuse those first couple of months (laughs). It was always going to take something special for me to leave the club and Celtic were the special opportunity I could not turn down.

You arrived at Celtic in 2000. The team had finished twenty-one points behind Rangers in the season prior to your arrival. Did that faze you in any way when you considered the move to the club?

Yes! The answer is yes. Absolutely, I was concerned. I have to admit that. There was nothing in pre-season in Germany and Ireland that convinced me otherwise. I had a definite concern and held on to the hope that if I could add a couple of players that the tide could steadily turn.

I would have been happy if Mark Viduka stayed at the club because he was a very good striker but when he departed, I knew that I wanted to sign Chris Sutton from Chelsea as his replacement. Honestly, signing Chris and his contribution in my first season was massive to us. He settled down and he instantly became a big player for the team and an excellent foil for Henrik Larsson.

Henrik loved playing with Chris and vice versa. Bringing Chris to the football club gave us the lift that we needed because had we not signed him at that time then we may not have beaten Rangers 6-2 early on in the season. Things could have been very different had that not happened.

Mind you, while we are talking about Chris, I would like to point out that he told me that he would never go into punditry and now he is doing it (laughs). But joking aside, he was brilliant for the club and a big landscape changer for me.

Was the 6-2 win over Rangers in only your fifth league game in charge of the club, the first time that you felt that you could achieve something special in your first season at Celtic?

At the time, even after that game, I thought that it was too early to make that assessment. With hindsight, as Celtic fans like yourself point out to me, that might have been the moment that there was a changing of the guard. It might have been.

Rangers did defeat us 5-1 around November time which was a blow but even then, I felt that we had built an inner strength as a team to see us through any troubled waters that were to arise in our way. From there, we went on to win the league title by fifteen points which was an incredible achievement for everyone.

You became the first Celtic manager since Jock Stein to win a domestic treble at Celtic. You did so in your first season in charge. Can you put into words how special that was for you?

It was an exhausting season but an incredible season for the club. The first time that I felt that we could win a treble, or at least that we could be in contention to do so, was after we won the League Cup final against Kilmarnock in March of that season. We were ahead in the league and after winning our first trophy together, I felt that we could go on and achieve the Scottish cup as well.

It was absolutely fantastic that we went on to do just that. However, as you know, the amazing thing in Scotland is that even after winning a treble, you do not get any real time to dwell on it and bask in your own glory because the focus immediately shifts to the next season and whether you can do it all over again. As well as being a rewarding season, it was also a mentally exhausting season for me and I took a short holiday of around seven to ten days to relax before getting back to fully focusing on the job that was to come in the next season.

Your recruitment at Celtic is considered to be strong with the likes of Chris Sutton, John Hartson, Alan Thompson and Neil Lennon signed. However, you also inherited three top-class players in Henrik Larsson, Paul Lambert and Lubomir Moravcik. Where like almost like a godsend for you as a manager?

They absolutely were like a gift from God for me.

Lubo Moravcik is the best two-footed player that I ever worked with. Without question. He could go either side and he did not have a weaker foot. I got to work with him when he was around thirty-three years of age. He was such a talent that I honestly think that if he had been around twenty-seven when we played Porto in Seville in the UEFA Cup final then there is no doubt that we would have won the match. I have no doubt about that. He would have sprinkled all sorts of magic over Seville. I genuinely believe that. Porto had some great players, but Lubo could have dealt with anything that was thrown at him and he would have caused Derlei and co all sorts of problems.

Paul Lambert was a great player and one who did well for Celtic and for me, but he also did very well for himself. To go from St Mirren and Motherwell to trials in Germany and earn a move to Dortmund before going on to win a European Cup is nothing short of remarkable.

Then you get Henrik Larsson who was nothing short of sensational. A great all-round footballer and a great goal scorer. Brave as a lion and someone who could play with different strike partners as he did with either Chris Sutton or John Hartson. It is no wonder that he is revered by Celtic fans. He is as good as you can get. The pleasing thing for me is that he left Celtic to join Barcelona and play a key role in their European Cup success of 2006, before playing at Manchester United in his late thirties. He showed that he could perform on the biggest stages in European football, in La Liga and in the Premier League. A remarkable talent.

Overall, how did you manage the aforementioned high-profile players that you had at Celtic. Did you try and simplify things as Brian Clough had done for you in your own playing career?

That is it. I allowed these kinds of players the scope to play. When you do that, you get it back tenfold. Allow them to play their natural game and create an environment that allows them to succeed by having ample depth across the squad to support them which I did also.

Do not confuse them with too much information. They did not need that. They needed encouragement and man management which is what Sir Alex did so well at Manchester United with players like Eric Cantona. Players like that need to be allowed to go and play. That is what I aimed to do and the rest followed in terms of trophies and success due to their ability to perform.

You left Celtic in 2005 for family reasons before returning to management over a year later with Aston Villa. You were so close to taking the club to the Champions League during your time in charge. What are your main memories from your time at the Villans?

It was another really good time in my career. My aim was to take the club into the Champions League. We were competing against the likes of Manchester United under Sir Alex, Chelsea under Mourinho and Arsenal under Wenger so it was difficult because they had bigger budgets than we had.

However, that did not stop us aiming for the top four. We went close in two seasons and qualified for the UEFA Cup which was great, but the Champions League is where we wanted to be.

We were also close to winning the League Cup in 2010 against Manchester United which I believe we would have done had the referee sent off Nemanja Vidic for a last-man challenge. We won a penalty, but he was only booked which I believe was wrong. Vidic should have gone and who knows what could have happened. It would have been lovely to win something with Aston Villa but as I say, Champions League was the aim.

You managed the Republic of Ireland from 2013 to 2018 and qualified for Euro 2016. You raised eyebrows by hiring Roy Keane as your assistant. What inspired that decision?

I had worked with Roy at ITV whilst they were covering Champions League football, so we got to know each other over the course of a few years. We talked about the possibility of working together should I return to management in the future if he was available. We did not think too much more into it than that then the Ireland job became available and I asked Roy to join me and I was delighted when he did.

Roy was manager in his own right and he was never short of giving an opinion, but he would go with my opinion even if we disagreed which made things work. Roy was excellent to work with and the players knew him as a player, and he was a strong influence on the group which was great.

How did managing at a major international tournament compare with playing at such a tournament?

When we got to France in 2016, it was great. It was like a dream really because I had seen the old footage of Jack Charlton leading Ireland at a major tournament and the scenes that came with it. I wanted to recreate some good moments for the fans because they follow the team everywhere and thankfully, we could do that during the tournament.

We had thousands of fans supporting us in France and beating Italy thanks to Robbie Brady scoring a brave header which is the highlight, for sure.

The big difference from playing to managing in such a tournament was the fact that in the weeks building up to the tournament, you are doing all that you can to build not only a strong team but a strong environment around the place, too. Whereas, when you are a player, you are focused on your own individual performance and fitness in the build-up to a tournament. Both experiences were fantastic.

*****

Ron Atkinson
A manager is nothing without his players

As a player, Ron Atkinson was a one-club man, playing over five hundred times for Oxford United.

After retiring in 1971, Atkinson took over at non-league Kettering Town, before joining Cambridge United where he won the Fourth Division title in 1977.

A successful spell at West Brom followed, taking the club to third place in the First Division and reaching the quarter finals of the UEFA Cup.

In 1981 'Big Ron' became manager of Manchester United where he won the FA Cup twice before returning to West Brom.

Atkinson also managed Atletico Madrid, Sheffield Wednesday (twice), Aston Villa, Coventry City and Nottingham Forest, winning the League Cup with both Wednesday and Villa.

You joined Manchester United in 1981. Can you sum how you felt when you were offered the job and what are your overriding memories of your time as Manchester United manager?

Manchester United is a massive football club as everyone around the globe knows. However, back then, my West Brom side were finishing higher than Manchester United. The club had won only one trophy in around twelve years with FA Cup success in 1977. It is important for younger fans of football to remember that Manchester United had been relegated in 1974 as well. That may be unthinkable to people now but that was the reality of that time.

I spoke to the chairman as soon as I went in to the club and told him that we had to ensure that Manchester United became a European club again. We duly delivered that in every year during my time at the club and we never finished lower than fourth in the league. I loved my time in charge of the club and to win two FA Cups as manager fills me with unbelievable levels of pride.

The FA Cup was a massive deal then and to win it twice was truly special and meant a lot to the club and myself. Unfortunately, the FA Cup has been diluted in the modern game which I think is a great shame.

For example, I would much rather win the FA Cup than finish fourth in the Premier League, but I doubt most modern-day managers would agree with that due to the finances. That is sad because football is all about the glory and the memories of lifting silverware. It certainly was for me. The only way to resolve it for me is to award the FA Cup winner a place in the Champions League. You would not see any managers playing reserve teams then I can assure you.

During your era in charge at Old Trafford, FA Cup finals could go to replays and that was the case in 1983 when you won the FA Cup for the first time. How did you handle that scenario as a manager and keep your group of players calm, having to play a showpiece final all over again?

We knew that we should have won the final in the first game so that ensured that we did not have any nerves or worry that we were not capable of winning. I told the players in the dressing room after Brighton equalised late on in the first final to force the replay, that if we played to our maximum in the replay that they would not stand a chance.

I was proven right as we won 4-0 and cruised through the game and led by three goals at halftime. We should have done that in the first final as we had that level of quality and confidence within the group. However, doing it in the replay did not change the fact that we won the trophy and it was ours on merit.

The second final in 1985 was completely different to the game in 1983. It was a tense game. Norman Whiteside made the difference for us on that occasion. Kevin Moran was sent off with just over ten minutes to go and my assistant Mick Brown said that we should shut up shop and play for a replay. I did not have it in me to do that. I told him that we'd keep three up front as I knew that we would win the game. I just had a feeling that day that we would beat Everton. We enjoyed our celebrations that night.

It was always a club rule of mine to make sure that the players fully enjoyed their successes. It was former Manchester United captain Noel Cantwell that told me early on in my managerial career that every success should be fully enjoyed to make sure that you want even more in future. So we certainly did that. We had a meal with the club after the first final which was a bit stuffy, to be honest. So, after the second final, I told Robbo (Bryan Robson) to take the boys away and have a great night which he duly did. That motto always worked well for me in management.

At Manchester United, you had so many big characters such as Bryan Robson, Norman Whiteside, Paul McGrath, Kevin Moran, Frank Stapleton as well as many others. How did you manage those players as individuals to get the best from them?

They were all easy to manage because they wanted to win. They wanted to be the best players that they could be. That is all a manager wants from his players.

Norman Whiteside. What a player he was to work with. People always talk Norman being aggressive and having that edge to his game, but he had so much awareness and ability as well. He does not get enough credit for that. When he received the ball, he could tell you where every player on the pitch was. Gordon Strachan told me when he arrived at the club that Norman might just be the best player that he had ever played with. That sums up how highly he was rated by me and his peers. His career sadly ended early due to injuries, but he achieved so much in a short time by winning cups at United, playing in World Cups and by making an impact on everyone he played with.

Paul McGrath was another who was special. I do not believe that there has been a better centre back in the Premier League than him. There have been many top centre backs but there have been none better than McGrath for me. He had it all.

I was fortunate to have very good players and it is always important to remind yourself that a manager is nothing without his players.

*****

Paul Tisdale
The key to managerial longevity

During a playing career that ended prematurely due to injury, Paul Tisdale played for Southampton, Northampton, Huddesrfield Town, Bristol City, Exeter City and Yeovil Town.

Tisdale's first managerial role was with Exeter, whom he joined in 2006. He spent twelve years at the helm before spells at MK Dons, Bristol Rovers and Stevenage.

You joined Exeter City as manager in 2006 and managed the club until 2018. A remarkable length of time in the modern game. From 2006 to 2009, you took the club from the Conference to League One, winning back-to-back promotions for the first time in Exeter history. Could you sum up your memories of that particular spell in charge of the club?

I had no career plan. I've just taken every season as it comes. When I went in to Exeter, my overriding goal was not to fail because over fifty per cent of first-time managers who leave their post never get another opportunity in management.

My priority as a coach was not to lose two games in a row because two defeats can very easily become three or four which can lead to you losing your job. I went over a hundred games before I lost two in a row.

I always made sure that I made it clear to the players from day one that they were my players. I've never agreed with the notion that a manager can go into a football club and state that the players that he has inherited aren't his. It is very easy to say to the press and the fans that you can only be judged when you have your 'own' squad. That for me is a cop out because I believe that the moment you sign a contract with a club that you accept the players that the club has as yours and do all that you can to work proactively with them.

I told the Exeter squad in 2006 on day one that they were my players and that everyone would be given an opportunity to impress me and my staff. I signed a couple of players and within eighteen months, I had then put my own stamp on it and got the team playing as I ideally wanted them to. Up until that point, I was pragmatic and business-like.

Then from around 2007 to 2011, I had the team playing in a pattern that I really wanted us to play. However, in 2011, that changed as we finished seventh in League One — which was and still remains Exeter's highest ever league finish — and we started to lose players to other clubs.

That changed the way that I could work as our players attracted the attention of big clubs who could afford to prize them from us.

It was an amazing first five years with the promotions from the National League to League One then it became a rebuilding process when I needed to build a new team.

You talk about rebuilding a team and during your twelve years with Exeter, you built numerous sides during a period of real stability for the club. What is the key to successful recruitment in your opinion and how do you adapt as a manager to promotion when you then need to build a squad to compete at a higher level?

That's a very broad question. First of all, it is important to acknowledge that every moment is different. There is no magical formula that will always work for you. Good recruitment stems from knowing your environment, the personalities of your squad and ensuring that you optimise player potential to the maximum.

For example, at Exeter, we had to compete against other clubs in our league with a smaller budget. Therefore, we had to get sufficiently good players at less of a price than our competitors in order to be competitive. That means that you need to make compromises and target players who have not yet reached their potential elsewhere or that you believe can play at a higher level than they currently are playing at.

Recently, a few high-profile pundits have stated that 'a leopard doesn't change its spots' in relation to footballers and their inner make up. I disagree with that as I believe that if you put a player into a healthy environment then you can change the application and perspective of a player.

At Exeter, we knew exactly what we were as a club which helped create a healthy working environment. We knew that it was a priority for us to develop our own players from the academy, sign talent on a comprise as I've discussed or older professionals at the latter end of their career to come in and set standards for the younger pros.

Twelve years is a long time to spend at one club in the modern game. How did you continually motivate yourself and strive for improvement year upon year within the same environment?

Sport can be very fluid with many athletes and staff members not setting down roots at one place for an extended period of time. In order to succeed over a long period of time, you have to be fully committed to the project and to be the best version of yourself in order to inspire those around you to continually improve too. That can be rare in football at times as people can look out for themselves and strive to make as much money as they can as quickly as possible.

I was aligned to the way that Exeter as a club functioned and I enjoyed my job. Motivation was never once a factor for me during my time at the club. I loved working with my colleagues, developing players and striving to create something unique. I was completely sold on building something very different.

I was offered many jobs during my time at Exeter and I turned them down because my burning ambition was to build Exeter as a club to one day play in the Championship. There aren't many bigger challenges than that and my form of ambition may be different to others who would have looked for a next move but that was not what I wanted.

Being as creative as a coach always kept me on my toes as we went through different cycles over the twelve years with players moving on which always brings a new set of challenges. Every season was different and I had to change the style that we played to suit the players that I had at my disposal. I enjoyed analysing data analytics to pinpoint improvement for my players and my staff.

For example, in my last two seasons with the club, I sold my front three who were integral to our 4-3-3 system and replaced them with one target man which led to me changing a new team and a new way of playing. Both seasons saw us reach eighty points and get to the play-offs but involved a different set of tactical principles. Changes like that always kept me incredibly motivated and interested as a coach as I loved the challenges of the job.

*****

Dick Campbell
The changing landscape of management

Dick Campbell made almost two hundred and fifty appearances as a player for Dundee United, Cowdenbeath, Dunfermline, Ross County, Brechin City and East Stirlingshire.

Since hanging up his boots in 1983, Campbell has accrued more than a thousand games as either manager or assistant with Cowdenbeath, Dunfermline, Brechin City, Partick Thistle, Ross County, Forfar and Arbroath. He has won multiple promotions, as well as the Third Division, League Two and League One titles.

You started managing in the 1980s. As we head into your fifth decade in management, did you think you would still be managing now and what has changed over your decades in management?

So much has changed. Let me ask you a question: do you think football has been enhanced by the hierarchy of the sport over the years? Because I will be honest and tell you that I do not think so.

Thank God we don't have VAR in Scotland. The game has changed in terms of systems, the speed of the game and I think we all need to be careful and conscious of the product that we are serving up.

On the positive side, players are far more fitter now than they ever were and they are technically better in my opinion too. I do miss some of the physicality that we had in the game and I think the crowds miss that too in all honesty.

I always think that there is far too much football on the telly these days. It is on seven days per week even on a Saturday night for goodness sake. When I played, our season ended in early April and did not start again until August. Whereas now we finish at the end of May and our first game is in the first week of July. That is not enough of a break. Referees, players, managers, coaches, directors and fans all need a break. Writers like you also need a break (laughs)! The footballing authorities need to have a serious think about the calendar.

I'll be brutally honest and admit that it does sometimes frustrate me that I've been in the game for over fifty years — as have others — and no one chaps on my door to ask me what I think about the state of football and how we could improve it. There are a lot of experts now in the game who have only been around for what feels like five minutes making major decisions and that can annoy me.

Well, let me ask you the question now, what do you think of the state of football and how can we improve it?

We need to always remember that football is a working-class communal sport. It always has been and always will be. If you are working hard all week and bringing up a family then football can be your escape from reality for a few hours at the weekend.

In my opinion, in my area based on what I see when driving past playing fields, girls seem to have taken the initiative to play sports and develop more than boys have. The playing fields where I live are regularly filled with girls football and rugby teams. They are out there and working hard which means that they are only going to continually improve and develop. I commend them and the development of female sport in Scotland.

I want to see more of that from young boys. When I was young, we would get home from school and throw the school bag down, grab a ball and head straight out to play football for hours. For example, even if it was as simple as hitting a ball against a wall. The harder you hit it, the better you would learn to control the ball. You just don't see enough of that anymore.

We need to get boys and girls of all ages playing football as much as possible because if we strive to develop the highest quality of player possible then we can get the crowds back to stadiums outside the Premiership.

I also think we need to improve the times that we play football. We need to stop being daft with scheduling by playing so many games at Christmas and New Year and in the middle of winter. We all have families and want to spend crucial time with them.

Stop playing games in the middle of winter and stop starting a new season a fortnight after the last season has ended. Give people a break to recharge and go again. We must be one of the only sports in the world that plays forty-eight out of the fifty-two weeks at all levels. It is unbelievable.

*****

Csaba László
Managing outside your comfort zone

Like so many managers, Csaba László was forced to retire from his playing career due to injury. He then moved into management, starting with Hungarian giants Ferencváros.

László has also managed many teams including, FC Sopron of Austria, the Ugandan national team, Hearts, Charleroi of Belgium, the Lithuanian national team, MTK Budapest and Dundee United.

You moved out of your comfort zone and left European football for African football in the mid-2000s. You managed the Uganda national team between 2006 and 2008. The Ugandan press nicknamed you 'The Miracle Man'. How would you sum up your experience of football in Africa?

I took the country from a hundred-and-eighty-first in the world rankings to ninety-first. We beat countries such as Nigeria and Angola for the first time in Uganda's footballing history and we just missed out on qualification for the African Cup of Nations.

It was such a unique experience. Uganda is a football-crazy country. The continent of Africa has many football-mad countries and I think that's underplayed as most of the world's media focus on European football. There is a lot of quality throughout various leagues in Africa too.

Football is the number one sport in many countries. Living in Africa was something that I absolutely loved. The people were incredibly friendly and I admired their attitude and dedication to football and their country.

I stayed in Uganda for my period in charge of the nation. I was offered the opportunity to stay in a hotel, but I refused. I wanted to live like the people of Uganda, so I bought a normal house and fully integrated myself into the job and into society. I wanted the people to see me as an equal rather than the stereotypical white man arriving to coach in Africa because he knows more than you. That's why fully integrating myself into the culture was important to me. It was a privilege to manage the nation and try to make the Ugandan people proud of their team.

Many of our players played outside Uganda and the quality of player was very good. We had top players in David Obua and Ibrahim Sekagya to name just two.

I made many fantastic memories during my time there. All I wanted to do was help the players to improve and progress and we did that as a team during my two and half years in charge.

CHAPTER THREE
The team behind the team

Craig Brown
The role of an assistant manager

After spells with Rangers, Dundee and Falkirk, Craig Brown took the plunge and became manager of Clyde in 1977.

During his ten seasons there he won the Second Division title.

Following seven years in charge of Scotland under-21s, Brown became the manager of the national side in 1993, taking Scotland to the 1996 European Championships and the 1998 World Cup.

Brown was also manager of Preston North End, Motherwell and Aberdeen.

IT'S amazing how times have changed in the game of football.

Over sixty years ago I joined Rangers – then, as now, the top team in Scotland. The Christmas gift to the players each year was a framed team photograph (below) taken at the annual public trial, first team against reserves with an attendance of upwards of ten thousand. This was a thoughtful initiative because six decades later it is possible to identify players and staff as all were carefully named under the picture.

But who was the assistant manager? There wasn't one! Forty-two players in the squad but only three staff – manager Scot Symon, trainer Davie Kinnear and assistant trainer Joe Craven. At that time there was no qualified physiotherapist, as I found to my personal cost, and Joe took charge of the reserve team. Talk about multi-tasking!

A modern team photo confirms a massive transformation. The proliferation of staff is remarkable, but understandable to a point. A large support staff is now a sine qua non at the top level – assistant manager, first-team coach, goalkeeping coach, strikers' coach, throw-in coach, sport scientist, fitness coach, injury-prevention coach, match analyst, doctor, physiotherapist, masseur, dietician, psychologist, kit controller, player liaison officer... and many roles are duplicated. So an assistant is required to help the manager deal with staff as well as the players.

By appointing an assistant in the summer of 1967 Symon was conceding that his role was becoming more and more onerous. Why Davie White? As manager of part-time Clyde, White had his team in third place in the top flight in season 1966-67. His determination to learn about management had prompted him to travel with Celtic to Lisbon to observe them in the European Cup final and also to Nuremberg to watch Rangers in the European Cup Winners' Cup final against Bayern Munich.

Symon was impressed and although White's only Ibrox credentials were that he supported the club, the manager endorsed his appointment as assistant manager. It was apparent that White was recruited with succession planning in mind. It was hoped that he would grow into the mammoth task of becoming only the fourth manager in Rangers' near hundred-year history.

Four months later when Symon was unceremoniously sacked – shamefully in the opinion of many Rangers fans, after winning six Scottish League titles, five Scottish Cups, four League Cups, as well as reaching a European Cup semi-final and two Cup Winners' Cup finals – and his number two was appointed. White's timing was desperately unfortunate as the man in charge of their greatest rivals was the incomparable Jock Stein.

When the former assistant manager was struggling in the opening weeks of the 1968-69 season it was obvious that he needed help – an assistant! Rangers turned to one of the greatest names in the club's history, a Rangers man with an impeccable CV having already successfully managed Dundee and Partick Thistle, Willie Thornton.

The preponderance of playing and technical staff clearly confirms that a right-hand man is necessary. But what criteria are most applicable? Should he be a young, ambitious coach with succession planning in mind, or an experienced club legend to help a fledgling manager?

There is no definite answer. Before exploring the various selection possibilities for such an important appointment I must emphasise something about which I feel strongly. The word 'assistant' implies subordination in the role. When I hear managers consistently using the first-person pronoun, saying: 'I did this/that' or 'My players' rather than 'Our players', it rankles. Similarly, referring to 'My assistant' disappoints me; surely the word 'we' or 'colleague' is more respectful and inclusive.

When a game has been won I feel it should be 'we' that is used, whereas after losing it is more honourable to use the singular and to accept responsibility. Also, it is pleasing to hear a manager refer to his colleague by name in interviews.

Whether the assistant is a young aspiring manager or a wily old fox, it is extremely helpful if the two men are socially friendly as well as professionally united. It is generally only the manager who has any real profile with scant reference to his cohort. The fact is, though, that often they work, and move from job to job, in pairs. There are many examples from decades ago until the present day of men doing football management in tandem.

Well-known pairs include Busby and Murphy, Clough and Taylor, Wenger and Rice, Kendall and Harvey, Reid and Heath, Mourinho and Faria, Howe and Tindall, Hughton and Trollope, Dyche and Woan, Ancelotti and Clement, Warnock and Blackwell, Hodgson and Lewington, Silva and Sousa, Ranieri and Shakespeare, O'Neill and Robertson, Venables and Howe, Klopp and Buvac, Dalglish and Harford, Shankly and Paisley, Redknapp and Bond, Coleman and Kean, Tuchel and Michaels, Rodgers and Davies, Farke and Reimer, Smith and O'Kelly, Evans and Raynor, etc.

North of the border we have had many similar double acts: Stein and Fallon, Prentice and McLean, Shankly and Kean, Souness and Smith, Smith and Knox, Calderwood and Nicholl, Levein and Houston, Dalglish and Barnes, Jefferies and Brown, Wallace and Totten, Lennon and Kennedy, McInnes and Docherty, Gerrard and McAllister, Glass and Russell, and many more.

It would be difficult to take issue with my opinion of the best-ever manager on the planet – Sir Alex Ferguson. Over the years he had no fewer than nine assistants, six of them at Manchester United. There's no uniformity among them which would indicate that he had no one specific criterion for the appointment other than a totally committed work ethic similar to his own.

At his first club, East Stirlingshire, there was no official assistant. He worked on his own but elevated the status of two senior players, John Donnachie and Bobby McCulley. Then at St Mirren he had physio-assistant manager Ricky McFarlane, followed by two bright young guys, Pat Stanton and Willie Garner, at Aberdeen before he lured Archie Knox from the manager's job at Forfar to join him at Pittodrie.

When Sir Alex went to Manchester United in September 1986 his first, and arguably finest, acquisition was Knox. This formidable combination put United back on track. Working with the guru undoubtedly provides considerable kudos, so much so that other clubs wishing to tap into United's successes seek to appoint those who have inside experience of The Master at work.

Walter Smith was one such wise operator; when he was appointed manager of Rangers he managed to entice Archie back to Glasgow. Smith and Knox had unparalleled success at home and in Europe while the disappointed Old Trafford manager tried various permutations and characteristics such as attitude and temperament to replace the incomparable Mr Knox.

Seeking an assistant with contrasting skills and abilities Sir Alex appointed fine men such as Brian Kidd, Steve McClaren, Rene Meulensteen, Carlos Queiroz, Walter Smith and Mike Phelan. All departed for various reasons.

Knox, an outstanding exponent in every aspect of the game, was the choice of a number of clubs due to his acquired reputation with the best club in England and two of the best in Scotland. In addition to being the number two at Aberdeen, United and Rangers, he worked at Everton with Walter Smith, Coventry with Eric Black, Millwall with Mark McGhee, Bolton with Sammy Lee, Blackburn with Paul Ince, Livingston with Richard Gough and Motherwell, Aberdeen and Scotland with me. That's no fewer than twelve assistant appointments. A record, I suggest!

One component is vital for success. The assistant must respect the manager and be fiercely loyal to his boss. This is exemplified by the Real Madrid and former Everton management team as the father-and-son combination of Carlo and Davide Ancelotti is unique.

I was assistant to two managers, Willie McLean at Motherwell and Andy Roxburgh with the Scotland national team. I held both in high esteem as football people and human beings, so it was straightforward for me to assume the subordinate position.

When I became manager in my own right after eight years as an assistant, I had excellent cohorts as manager of Clyde. Ross Mathie and Rab Thorburn both had the necessary attributes of industry, loyalty, intelligence, diplomacy, determination, discipline, imagination, ambition and game-awareness.

While working as assistant to Andy Roxburgh I had charge of the Scotland Under-21 team, so I required reliable assistance. Tommy Craig, the former Aberdeen, Sheffield Wednesday, Newcastle, Aston Villa, Swansea, Carlisle and Hibernian midfielder, exemplified all the necessary qualities and could be left in charge when I was with the senior side.

I was extremely fortunate to have two outstanding colleagues in my eight years in charge of Scotland. The assistant's role was a part-time appointment, so it was possible for the selected incumbent to remain with his club and join the international squad for matches only.

My first right-hand man was the then-Hibernian manager, Alex Miller, who was very influential in the success we had in qualifying for Euro 96 and the 1998 World Cup.

When Alex left Hibs he went to work for Liverpool under Rafa Benitez who felt that at international-match gathering time Alex should remain at Melwood to coach young players such as Steven Gerrard, Jamie Carragher and Michael Owen. With reluctance Alex had to resign, and it was then my good fortune to appoint the doyen of assistants. . . Archie Knox.

We had a fruitful relationship which extended to further spells together at Motherwell and Aberdeen. When asked to account for his many different jobs, Archie's typical quip was: 'Keep on the move before they find you out!'

There is no standard job description for a manager's assistant, but often he is in charge of the training programme, collating opposition and recruitment reports, pre-match warm-ups and sharing the responsibility for team selection and the 'game plan' (which used to be called 'tactics').

I learned as an assistant to look closely at the opposition for the first ten to fifteen minutes of play and advise if there was any deviation from their predicted team shape. I instigated this good routine in my own set-up.

I also briefly discussed possible substitutions during the game and asked my colleague to watch the effort of each substitute as he warmed up and make a fuss of ensuring that his pulse was checked and was at least three-quarters of his maximum before allowing him to enter the fray.

Over the years I got to know that if a player had an axe to grind he was often more disposed to confide in the number two. However, I always made them aware when I was an assistant that my first loyalty was to the manager. I told them: 'Don't say anything to me that you don't want the boss to hear.'

Without having to hear it, a manager wants first and foremost loyalty and trust from his assistant, while the assistant wants to feel that his contribution is appreciated and valued.

*****

Rene Meulensteen
The reality of being first team coach

After a playing career spent in Holland, Meulensteen managerial roles in Qatar before joining Manchester United as first team coach in 2001. Over the next twelve years (that included a brief spell in charge of Brondby), he helped United win multiple trophies, including the Premier League, FA Cup and Champions League.

You coached at the elite level of football with Manchester United under Sir Alex Ferguson where you served as first team coach. How do you go about planning and evaluating coaching sessions at that level?

Due to the success of the team, we had such a stringent playing schedule as we were often playing deep into cup competitions in addition to our league games.

That meant that I was planning sessions to cover two or three games in advance as Sir Alex would always anticipate the type of line up that he wanted to play in advance of particular games.

My job first and foremost was to inform the players about the strengths and limitations of our upcoming opponents to ensure that they had a clear picture in their head about what they would be coming up against.

Things like style of play, formations or individual tactics such as long throws would come into that.

However, our main focus was to prepare the players to be able to play to our strengths and focus on how we would win any upcoming game.

I would plan and then facilitate our training sessions aiming to replicate scenarios that could play out on a match day.

Within that, repetition is key because you want to ensure that players achieve a level of success and confidence on the training ground that they could take into a game.

Overall, my coaching navigation system at Manchester United was quite straightforward.

I had a meeting with Sir Alex Ferguson when he promoted me to first team coach when he told me that I would have full responsibility for leading and implementing my sessions.

All that he asked for was that whenever we trained, he wanted to be able to see the best version of Manchester United in front of him.

In defence, he wanted us to be able to press teams high and with aggression with the caveat that our players would be as equally confident to be able to drop deep and absorb pressure when necessary.

Every scenario was based on the ability to be flexible and transition as quickly and as seamlessly as possible.

In midfield, he wanted United to always be confident in possession and able to take the initiative to any opponent.

The key to this is rhythm in your attacking training sessions that enables players to control the tempo of a game to their strengths. All of the best sides in world football are able to do this.

They can control the rhythm of a game and change it at any time too.

The speed of the game will dictate the number of touches you can have within a game. Players need to constantly be looking to break the lines of the pitch and continually ask tough questions of the opposition in defence.

Quality of possession and dictating the rhythm of a game leads to more time being spent in the final third of the pitch which in turn leads to more chances being created and goals being scored.

When you can score goals, you take more control of the game and from there, you can adapt your rhythm to further enhance your control of the game.

Controlling possession in such a way helps you maximise the number of chances that you create and the more goals you can score in that time is how you dominate your opponent and sustain success.

Finally, he emphasised that the attacking phase was the most important aspect of Manchester United's play to him.

He wanted us to attack with speed, power, penetration and unpredictability.

Those defensive, midfield and attacking ideals of play that Sir Alex held is what he demanded that I implement into every single training session.

Those principles were the key factors for me to be able to plan my sessions to ensure that we could use what the gaffer wanted to see to our benefit.

In addition to the ideals of play that Sir Alex held for his teams, I also had three key principles that revolved around all of my training sessions.

The first of those was to ensure that the players always understood the purpose of my training sessions. I had to inform the players in order to best facilitate them which goes back to what I said earlier. This process is vital when working with top class players.

Secondly, every training session had to incorporate a challenge within it to keep the players on their toes and keep each session fresh. That challenge could be anything from a particular physical challenge or a tactical challenge. Purposeful and challenging training have to go together.

Thirdly, within every training session, you must ensure that quality and intensity are interlinked in everything that you do.

You need to ensure that every is working towards their optimum level of quality and fitness in order to maintain the highest of standards.

Given that Sir Alex delegated to you a lot on the training field, how would that work on a match day itself? What would your specific role be on such occasions?

On the match day, you have to see the whole picture. During my sessions, I informed the players of what we were working towards and why, such as what our drills would be for each day on the training pitch and informing them of our opponent's strengths and weaknesses.

I would follow that up during the week with video analysis of around eight to ten minutes. Those sessions would be used by me to back up what I had already shared with them on the pitch about our opponent, i.e. their style, their key players and their weaknesses or unique tactical elements.

During the video session, I would also showcase examples of how other teams have caused our opponents problems to show the players it in action.

That would then lead to me focusing my sessions towards a match day on being all about us and what we had to do as a collective team effort in order to win the game.

The sessions at the end of the week would also be backed with a video analysis session to further emphasise that these would be the moments in the game that we are looking for.

On a match day itself, I would conduct a short recap video session at the stadium on a home match day or at the team hotel on an away match day.

This video session would be short and snappy to emphasise what we had done during the week, what we want to do in the game and because the team was named by this stage, I could also be very specific in naming names.

After that video session on a match day, Sir Alex would take over and speak to the players before sending them out to take to the pitch for the game.

During the game, I would speak to the manager on the bench. Then, at halftime, Sir Alex would address the team as a whole.

After that, I would speak to the midfielders and attackers to highlight what was going well and what we wanted to see more of or see differently in the second half. While I was doing this, Mike Phelan would be doing the same with our defensive players and Eric Steele with the goalkeeper.

That was the match day routine for me and for Sir Alex and the staff during my time as first team coach.

What are the main challenges as a coach when it comes to coaching elite level footballers?

The key is to inform them, facilitate them and allow them to take responsibility. You have to empower them in a sense. Players at the elite level do not need over coached. They do not need stop-stand-still sessions like you would do with players of the age of thirteen or fourteen, for example.

Your role is to create the right environment so that the players know what is happening and why so that you can then give any extra information to players on an individual basis.

For example, if we knew that our opponent struggled with switches of play then we would look to use that as a weapon of our in the game. In that example, I would have a chat with Paul Scholes and emphasise to him that switching the play to a particular side was something that he should prioritise during the game.

I would also set up drills that would mimic the opposition and their struggle to adapt to a switch of play to allow Scholes to get that muscle memory of where he wants to play the ball when it occurs in the game. I facilitate such a drill so that Scholes can do it during the game and paint the picture to complete the task.

As a coach, you must recognise that you are working with elite players and respect their quality by giving them the opportunity to take as much responsibility for their game as possible.

Finally, Rene, in addition to being a first team coach with Sir Alex Ferguson at Manchester United, you have also managed in the Premier League in your own right with Fulham. Readers may think that those roles are similar but many people within the game have spoken about the real differences between them. So, how do those roles differ in reality?

There is a difference, for sure. As a manager, you need to deal with every aspect of your squad, manage upwards by working with the CEO, sporting director and the owner as well as manage sideways with your assistants and the rest of your staff.

All eyes are on you and you must ensure that you delegate and work as a collective with your staff to best you prepare the team for a match day.

That is what made Sir Alex Ferguson so special. He had world class capabilities as his track record in football shows, but he also knew when and what aspects to delegate to his staff. You cannot do everything on your own.

Another key difference to being a manager is dealing with and managing the media, handling conversations with players and their agents and board members.

You do not need to worry about anything at that level when you are a first team coach but when you are a manager, those things are at the forefront of your inbox in addition to the preparation of the team.

Social media is also a massive factor on the game now. So many fans consume football via social media, so it has a presence within football now whether you like it or not.

Everyone especially the fans of your club are entitled to their opinions and they will not be shy in sharing them with you such is the nature of football and always has been the nature of football.

Sometimes, with social media, opinions are magnified further than they were in the past which can make things slightly more difficult for managers, coaches, staff and players alike because momentum is a tide that can be hard to turn when the wind blows in a certain direction.

For example, someone can say that player X or manager Y is the worst person to have ever worked for their club or whatever it may be.

They can say that via a keyboard with no consequences or real emotion whereas the people that face the consequences of such words are those who they write about.

Unfortunately, dealing with severe criticism and scrutiny is a tough reality that comes when you work in top level sport and as such having strong mental strength, belief in your ability and your philosophy of football are key components to being able to forge a career in the game in whatever role you work in.

*****

Jonathan Gould
The art of goalkeeping and coaching the next generation

The son of the former Wimbledon and Wales manager Bobby Gould, Jonathan Gould played for Halifax, West Brom, Coventry City, Bradford, Gillingham, Celtic, Preston, Hereford, and Bristol City. He also won two caps for Scotland.

After retiring, he turned his hand to coaching.

As a goalkeeper, you represented clubs such as Celtic, Bradford, Coventry and the Scotland national team. What are your personal highlights from your career in the game?

Appearing at Wembley in 1996 while I was at Bradford is a day that will live long in the memory. We beat Notts County 2-0 to win promotion which was an incredible moment for me professionally.

It was also an emotive moment for me personally as my father and my son as well as my wider family were all able to watch me play on that special day. That meant a lot.

My time at Celtic is also a time of my life that fills me with great pride. To represent a club of that magnitude and win trophies in front of thousands of special fans was unbelievable.

Stopping our rivals from winning ten in a row in the late 1990s stands out as being such an historic season for me and also for the club. Then, to go on from that to win a treble under Martin O'Neill in his first season at the club was also amazing to be a part of.

A career in football is defined by taking control of moments which present themselves to you and luckily, I was able to do that throughout my career.

The role of a goalkeeper is a specialist position and in my view, probably the most challenging position on the field as you are out on your own to some regard. How important is mentality as well as ability for a goalkeeper?

As a coach now, mentality is one of the first things that I look for in a goalkeeper. You need to have a presence and know how to keep yourself motivated and involved in a game that you are not necessarily called upon too often in. I learned this at two ends of the footballing spectrum at Halifax Town and Celtic.

At Halifax, I quickly learned what it took to be a busy

goalkeeper as I was called upon a lot in those days. Consistency was crucial to my game as it is for any goalkeeper in a team that concedes chances.

You need to constantly be on the top of your game to read situations and know how to communicate with your back four to maintain form without making too many mistakes.

Whereas, at Celtic, concentration was the key factor that would define my performance on a match day because I might only be called upon once in a game.

However, that one moment could be the difference between winning or losing. You always need to be prepared for something occurring out of nothing against the run of play.

David Seaman is a great example of how to maintain high standards at a major club due to his level of concentration which for the most part was exceptional. During the 1990s, he had a superb back four in front of him but even then, would still be called upon from time to time.

Communication is also vital in those moments as you have to be in sync with your back four to know when is the time to come off your line and be aggressive in gathering the ball and when is the time to trust those in front of you and remain at the heart of the goalmouth.

You have moved on from being a player to becoming a goalkeeping coach at club level and international level. What does the role of a goalkeeping coach look like on a daily basis?

It all depends on the situation that you are working within and the experience of the goalkeepers at the club.

For example, I was working as West Bromwich Albion's goalkeeping coach in the Premier League when Ben Foster, Boaz Myhill and Anders Lindegaard were the goalkeepers at the club.

I would describe my role in that situation to be similar to that of a caddy in golf. You have such a tight relationship with the players that you are working with as it's a small group and you know that your role is to provide them a maintenance programme by pushing them as much as you can whilst also offering advice when necessary.

I took that approach based upon working with Peter Latchford who was my coach at Celtic. He was great at predicting how a game would go and helping you know what was likely to come in a particular game.

He taught me that by using your experience of being involved in the game that a goalkeeping coach can prime their goalkeepers for what to expect in a given match.

Of course, there are anomalies to that rule. I have taken a side to Old Trafford and primed my goalkeepers for an exceptionally busy day and in the end, the run of play dictates that they have an unexpectedly quiet day. It does not always legislate as you plan but giving them as much information as you can is key.

The game has changed dramatically over the last few decades because of the amount of video analysis platforms that clubs have access to. As a coach, I can show my players, every goal or penalty that an opponent has had in the season to date.

I did not have that back in the late 1990s and early 2000s. I would have to record a match and fast forward and rewind the video of a full match to gather the relevant information that I needed whereas in the modern day that video can be cut into an easy to view package for the player.

All the information that we need regarding opposition teams is at our finger tips as coaches and can enable us to give our players as much detail as they feel is needed for any game that is coming up.

Goalkeepers' mistakes are always highlighted more than mistakes from outfield players as inevitably they tend to lead to more goals being conceded given the nature of the role.

How did you handle mistakes as a player and how do you support your players when they make an error as a coach?

As a player, I knew when I made a mistake that was costly or that I did not have an explanation for.

I would hold my hands up rather than try and explain myself. Accountability is a crucial aspect of goalkeeping because as you've said, when we make an error there is a higher percentage risk that it will lead to a goal being conceded.

Similarly, when it comes to coaching, I look for honesty and accountability within the goalkeepers that I am working with. Most of them generally get it.

Video analysis is a crucial driver for us to work on minimising mistakes because we can get four or five angles on each goal or passage of play. That enables us to work out what caused the error, whether that be the goalkeepers starting position or lack of adjustment.

Our role is to look for every minute detail to help the players that we coach regardless of their experience because even the very best of goalkeepers can make errors such is human nature.

You represented Scotland as a player at international level and you have experience of coaching at international level with New Zealand. Does your role as coach alter from club football to international football in any way?

The main adjustment is time because with the national side, I am only getting to work with the players for short bursts rather than prolonged periods like you have within club football.

Utilising platforms such as Wyscout is key to my role with the national team because I can access most leagues in world football on the platform which enables me to analyse our national team goalkeepers who may be playing in different parts of the world.

For example, with New Zealand, I had goalkeepers who we were monitoring for each squad playing in six different leagues across the globe.

In that situation, my role is to do watch their matches and do a weekly review of their performances for the national team coach in order to give him all of the information required to make an informed choice ahead of choosing his latest squad.

When I watch a game, I always aim to gather as much detail as possible so that I can provide a thorough report for the national team with no stone uncovered.

I will look at things such as the actions that the goalkeeper has within a game, the number of distributions that they have and any goals that are conceded and what the causes were.

Maintaining contact with your players is another aspect of working at national team level that is important. I may not see each goalkeeper in person for two to three months, so it is important to communicate whether that be over the phone or via Skype.

It is important that the players know that we are there for them even if it is just to be a sounding board because they are going through a challenging time at club level in the side or by not playing as much as they would like to.

I call on my personal experiences because I was capped twice by Scotland but spent thirty or so games on the bench, so I know how that feels for a goalkeeper.

In regard to second or third choice goalkeepers, how important is it as a coach to keep them on their toes in case they are called upon unexpectedly within a game?

It is a factor that has to be taken into account as a coach.

For example, at West Brom, we had Ben Foster who was always fit and played at a high standard most weeks. We also had Boaz Myhill who is a tremendous goalkeeper and a top character.

Boaz knew that whenever Ben was fit that he was most likely going to play and he would be the first to admit that he had little moments where he could have looked after himself better but that is where I come in as a coach to make sure that I push him and leave no room for complacency. Not that there ever really was with Boaz.

I know how it feels because at Celtic, I was in the exact same position that Boaz was in at West Brom and I could also have looked after myself a little better at times.

It comes down to personal pride for any second or third choice goalkeeper because even though you are aware that is unlikely that you will play many games, you should never want to let yourself down or give up on pushing for a place in the team. You must always maintain belief in yourself.

You just never know how quickly things can change and I explain that to the players that I work with because I was third choice goalkeeper at Bradford and then found myself moving to Celtic as their number one goalkeeper in a matter of months. Therefore, you must always be readily prepared because you are an injury or a move away from being the man who is relied upon between the posts.

Your father Bobby was a successful manager, you played and now coach at a high level and your son Matthew is a goalkeeper who has been involved at international level too. The game of football has evolved throughout the generations that your family has been involved within it. How do you see the game evolving for goalkeepers in the future given what you've witnessed with the game so far?

The game has evolved massively. I started when the back pass rule was not introduced so I could pick the ball up from one of my own players passing back to me.

The back pass rule was then introduced in the early 1990s when I was at Halifax and that changed the way that game was viewed and it also impacted on goalkeepers as it changed our approach.

I go into football clubs now and the goalkeeper is now seen almost like an outfield player with what is expected from them on the ball. I think that will continually grow and evolve in the coming years.

Despite that, it is my view that the crux of goalkeeping is still defined by quality decision making and positioning to be able to use the right technique to keep the ball out of the net no matter how unorthodox that may look.

Producing technically efficient goalkeepers is something that is a positive development, but we must never get away from the fact that the goalkeeper for any side is there to prevent goals being conceded.

Maybe I am old fashioned but for me that should always be the primary aim of any goalkeeper.

*****

Gary Lewin
The day to day reality of physiotherapy in football

Gary Lewin played in Arsenal's youth team before first-team physio in 1986, a role he held for twenty-two years. He also spent over twenty years as physio for the England national team.

Before we discuss your experiences with club and country first hand, I want to start by asking specifically about your roles. You have been a physiotherapist and head of medical services in your illustrious career. What do those roles look like within football on a daily basis?

Basically, you are working seven days per week making sure that you are available twenty-four hours each day to be at the beck and call of the players and the staff. It is a very demanding job that takes up the majority of your time, so you have to be dedicated to it.

For example, I had my first Christmas Day with family in twenty-five years when I left Arsenal in 2008 because we would train on Christmas Day every year before staying at a hotel on the evening of Christmas. We'd also play on New Year's Day so I was always unavailable on New Year's Eve and it was only permitted to take holidays in June when the club season was over so the job does impact your family life.

However, you make those tough sacrifices because it is a job that you love and it's very rewarding to be working hands-on at the elite level of sport.

You joined Arsenal as a first-team physiotherapist in 1986 and served under managers such as George Graham and Arsene Wenger in a twenty-two-year association with the club. What are the standout memories that you have from that period?

George Graham brought me into Arsenal, so I have very fond memories of George and what he achieved at the club. The club were in a very low period before George arrived and he reformed the club. He got rid of some of the so-called stars of Arsenal and replaced them with exciting academy players bound by an incredibly strong work ethic.

He was very demanding, but he got the best out of the players and everyone in the club by being that way. We won the League Cup in 1987 beating Tottenham on the way to the final. We won the league title at Anfield in 1989 which will always be the pinnacle of my career. We won the league again in 1991, we won a League Cup and FA Cup double and then capped it all off by winning the Cup Winners' Cup against Parma.

Those were fantastic years, and it was very sad that George left the club under controversial circumstances because he gave the club so much and he was always very good to me during my time working for him.

Many within football believe that Arsene Wenger revolutionised

the physical performance of players at Arsenal, which then influenced English football as a whole. How closely did you work with Arsene in those early years of his era to ensure that he settled the players into his way of thinking as soon as possible?

Arsene was great. He involved the staff from day one and was very clear at explaining what he wanted to achieve. He revolutionised each player's approach to training and preparation which was influenced by sports science.

Before Arsene, there was an attitude in English football that as long as you won on a Saturday then what you did for the rest of the week didn't really matter, whereas Arsene always emphasised that you should train as you play and prepare your body as best as you possibly can for maximum progression.

The food provided around the club changed, the intensity of each training session changed and our matchday preparation changed as we would stay in a hotel before every match regardless of whether it was home or away.

You worked with the England National team from 1996 to 2017. How proud were you to work for the national side and did you have to liaise with physiotherapists at club sides to aid your work during international breaks?

I worked for the national side on a part-time basis only during international breaks for the first twelve years while I worked at Arsenal for the remainder of the time. That was difficult to manage as it was very time consuming, and I was liaising with clubs while also being a full-time employee of Arsenal.

That changed in 2008 when I left Arsenal and moved to work with the national team on a full-time basis. This enabled me to go around all of the clubs and check in with the medical staff of each club and the players on a hands-on basis.

It was the greatest honour to work for England. Whenever I hear the national anthem, it gives me goosebumps as reminds me of each game that I was on the sideline for and even though we were unable to win anything, I still look back with immense pride at working for my country.

You went to nine major tournaments with the England national team. What is it like working at a major tournament with the eyes of the nation on every movement of the squad during that period?

You are living in a goldfish bowl for those five or six weeks of the tournament. You block off much of what is going on in the outside world as your full focus is on what you are striving to achieve within the camp. Being so close to everyone within the camp creates a family atmosphere. You are living and breathing football every single day with the same group of players and staff. Whenever a tournament ends it is always a very sad moment as you have spent so much time around each other that it becomes the norm.

Even now if I meet a player that I was on a tournament with it is like meeting a family member. There are mental and physical challenges to each tournament, but you also realise just how much of an honour it is to be in that role.

Finally, what advice would you give to any budding physiotherapists or medical personnel who would like to work within the football industry?

I would advise them to be aware that it is a very demanding job with long hours but one that is also very rewarding. There are thousands of qualified medical staff who want to get into sport, so my main piece of advice to those striving to get into the industry is make yourself stand out.

Volunteer to work evenings and weekends, strive to deepen your knowledge with post-graduate qualifications and gain as much experience as you can across sports, whether that's at the local football, rugby or cricket club because every experience matters and counts.

*****

Les Ferdinand
The realities of being director of football

Les Ferdinand started his career playing for non-league Hayes, before signing for First Division QPR In 1997.

During his time at Loftus Road, Ferdinand scored almost

a hundred goals which earned him a big-money move to Newcastle United.

As well as earning seventeen caps for England, he also represented Tottenham Hotspur, West Ham, Leicester City, Bolton, Reading and Watford.

After hanging up his boots, he returned to Spurs as coach and later became Director of Football at QPR.

You were an esteemed footballer who represented England and clubs such as Tottenham Hotspur, Queens Park Rangers and Newcastle United during your career. You have since become a highly respected director of football at Queens Park Rangers. Can you describe how that transition occurred as well as the initial learning process of becoming a sports director?

The transition happened following retirement when I took up coaching at Tottenham after I earned my coaching badges.

I also did some media work and combined that with coaching at Spurs with the youth teams then under Harry Redknapp.

While I was doing that, I thought carefully about becoming a manager and ultimately concluded that I did not want to go down that path as it is a precarious job in the current era of football.

Not too many former players move from playing into the director of football role and I felt that former players could excel in that role given their experiences within the game so that motivated me to pursue my qualifications in that particular field.

I studied a course in applied management towards the end of my playing career at Warwick University. The experience of studying at Warwick gave me a strong indication of what it would be like to go into a directorial role within football and from there I pursued opportunities to further develop myself in that field upon retirement.

In your experience as a director of football, what does the role entail on a daily basis at a football club?

The role is multi-faceted and requires dedication due to the level of detail that you are responsible for within a club.

I studied on a CPD course at the FA with other sporting directors and it became apparent quickly within our meetings that the role means different things at different football clubs depending on the directive that comes from the ownership of a club.

Player recruitment is the thing that many fans immediately associate with the role and that does play a part as you are involved in negotiations with players and their representatives and in discussions with your manager as to the type of players that he wants to pursue.

In my experience at QPR, recruitment is part of my role, but we also have a dedicated scouting team and a head of recruitment employee who go out and find the players that we require.

If the scouting department and the head of recruitment agree on a player then it comes to the manager and myself for the final say.

My job is to present the manager with four or five options in a given position and work with him to pinpoint the one that he wants for the football club.

I do not pick the players for the manager in my role. The manager has to be heavily involved in the process and it is my job to liaise with him to work together on securing the right players to progress the football club in the right direction.

Aside from recruitment, the youth academy is also part of my remit and I have revamped the structure at the club over the years in the academy at QPR with the aim of creating a realistic pathway at the club for our young players.

Working with the medical and sports science teams is also a crucial aspect of my role so that I have a clear understanding of what is going on in all aspects of the club in regards to the playing staff.

In your role, you mention working with the manager as being a key component of your job. How do you personally go about doing that?

It is a partnership approach. The manager has to work in harmony with the director of football at any club and that is my aim as a director of football. We have to support one another.

Being at loggerheads would make things chaotic. However we do not have to agree on everything as debate is healthy within any organisation that is striving to make progress.

Mutual respect is at the heart of that relationship and I want to support any manager that I work with in order for them to have the best possible chance of success for the football club.

Success and progression is the ultimate aim for me and for the manager. His role is to get results on a Saturday and my role is to look at the club in a holistic manner to try and ensure that all aspects of the club are in good shape to give him the opportunity to do that.

Last but not least, specialised coaches such as set-piece coaches have come into the game more and more over the last decade. In your role, is this something that you see as a positive development and something that will continue in the years to come for football club?

I see it as a positive because you want to give the team the best chance of success. We can learn from different sports and specialised coaches have been prevalent in the NFL, as an example, for many years.

It is important that football learns from other sports too and is not focused on being insular and only thinking of what has come before.

As a director of football, you need to consider everything that could help strengthen your club and that is what I have always looked to do.

I am always looking to continually learn and develop in my role too because you can always learn from others within your sport or from other sports or sectors of society too.

CHAPTER FOUR
Refereeing the game

Keith Hackett
Prepare, file and forget: My life as a referee

Keith Hackett began his football league career in 1972 as a linesman. Four years later he became a referee – a role he held for almost twenty years.

During his time as 'the man in the middle' Hackett refereed FA Cup finals, Chairty Shields and he was England's representative at the 1988 European Championships and the 1988 Olympic Games.

The focus of football fans and media companies ahead of any game is on the preparation of the players and the managers of each club. However, the man or woman in the middle has to prepare too. How did you prepare for a game in the days leading up to it and on the day of the match itself?

Firstly, I had to make a judgment what time I would need to leave home/office in order to arrive at the ground well before kick-off.

I would aim to arrive at 1pm for a 3pm kick off at the latest. I would build into my journey usually travelling by car a break to have some food and refreshments,

During my career we did not receive any advice on fitness regimes and nutrition. We simply developed our own routine.

My pre-match meal around noon would be two poached eggs on toast with a black coffee. I would have packed my own kit on the Friday before a game.

During my career we were discouraged to stay in hotel accommodation so if I had an appointment in London, it would be an early start travelling by car the one hundred and eighty plus miles.

I would do a small amount of research into the two teams, their recent history and position in the league. I would try to find out how the game went the last time the two teams met.

When I was appointed general manager of the Professional Game Match Officials, I made some dynamic changes which included, fitness regimes, pre-match warm up, nutrition advice and in depth preparation of the teams thanks to Prozone Referee Analysis.

What was your mindset when you were refereeing in the game?

I would spend a lot of time talking to myself trying to bring forward enhanced cognitive skills. I was always confident but worked hard to ensure that I avoided coming across as arrogant.

I prepared thoroughly with my two linesmen (now called assistant referees) to ensure that we were a strong team, supporting each other. Football is a team game for each club and for match officials it is no different. We work as a team to maximise our performance and all we want to do is ensure that the match that we are officiating can run as smoothly as possible for the players, managers, staff and, of course, the supporters.

How did you manage big personalities on the pitch and in the dugout. Did you have a particular strategy?

I was honoured to be on the same pitch and treated them with respect in the hope that it would be returned. Those difficult players were managed effectively through good COMMUNICATION, CONTROL, CONFIDENCE, COMMONSENSE. I was the referee with the best seat in the house.

Mistakes happen in any walk of life however any mistake made by a high-profile referee is arguably more amplified than any other profession. How did you handle mistakes and evaluate your performance?

File and forget. Referees are human and there is not a referee that has not made a mistake. During the game you have to forget it quickly and move on. Post match is the time to analyse performance and if you think that an error has been made you have to determine how you avoid it.

The simple formula is the more games you referee the better you become if you have a good process of reviewing your games and finding ways to improve.

*****

Stuart Dougal
Balancing working life with elite level refereeing

During his may years as a referee, Stuart Dougal officiated over a hundred international fixtures, including two European Finals. He also refereed the Scottish Cup Final in both 2004 and 2008.

As a referee, preparation is key as Keith has discussed. You had the privilege of refereeing numerous show piece cup finals and high-profile games at club and international level in your career. Did you ever change your normal preparation for such events or were your required to change your preparation due to security concerns?

In the main, I tried to keep to my usual preparations as much as possible in terms of diet and training leading up to the bigger, show piece, matches. However, I had to adapt for games such as a National Cup Final or Champions League match midweek as there was greater security around these matches. The main thing though was keeping a sharp focus for the game in hand.

Mistakes happen for people in all walks of life. Evaluation is an important step of the learning process for children and adults of all ages.

How did you evaluate your performance as a referee personally and in partnership with an examiner?

I used to record my matches but as time progressed, we were usually given a DVD of the match before leaving the stadium and this enabled me to review my performance soon after the game had ended. I was very self-critical (I think you have to be to continually improve) and regular dialogue with those whose opinions I valued, be it former referees or colleagues who were officiating too, was a must for me. In terms of the supervisor's evaluation, for games in Scotland, that took place over the phone a day or two after the match. However, for European matches the evaluation was much more immediate and it was done an hour or two after the match had concluded. This, depending on how the game had gone, had an effect on how much we enjoyed the rest of the evening!

You later took on punditry roles upon retiring as a referee. What was it like being on the other side of the fence? Did you find it tough to be fully objective at times due to your hand experience of the pressures that your colleagues were under?

I enjoyed trying to put forward the thinking of a match official whether that was in a weekly column I did for a Scottish newspaper or being interviewed on television whenever there were incidents worthy of further scrutiny. In my experience, many fans wanted to hear the facts from those at the sharp end, especially when it concerned the actual Laws of the Game and not necessarily just an opinion on whether a foul had been committed or not. That's why I enjoyed the role at BT Sport as I could help the pundits with the factual laws but not compromise them having their own opinions on incidents. In Scotland, all referees are part time and have a day job to support them as well as their career in football.

How did you manage the work-life balance during your career and what were the main challenges of being a high-profile person within football at work or when socialising?

Simply, I couldn't have managed that without the support of my wife as we had two young girls as I was making my way in the game or my employers as the demands on refereeing at the top level are huge.

A lot of time (almost daily) is spent training out-with your normal business hours as well as travelling to and from games. A European match was a minimum of three days away from home/work and domestically, for SPL games, we had to meet around three hours before kick-off which made your day quite long, especially for midweek games. In terms of socialising, I was never one for going down the pub for a pint but did a lot of entertaining in my 'day job'. However, again, in the main, I found most fans to be interested to meet a referee and talk over decisions and hear about some of our experiences.

CHAPTER FIVE
The media and their role covering the game

Oliver Kay
Football writing and ground hopping

Oliver Kay is a senior writer at *The Athletic*. He previously spent almost twenty years working at *The Times*. Oliver is also the author of *Forever Young: The Story of Adrian Doherty, Football's Lost Genius*.

You have covered live matches for a number of outlets during your career in football thus far. How do you typically prepare for a game that you are covering?

When I was first starting out in the late 1990s, I would spend hours poring over books to make sure I had every player's age and background, all the stats about their season and career, what both managers had said in the build-up etc.

That changed over the years as I found myself constantly going from one game to the next, often coming straight from a press conference or an interview and racing to get there in time. (Shamefaced confession: my timekeeping is — or possibly was — terrible.) When you're spread too thin, as has been the case with me at times in my career, it can be hard to prepare properly for every match.

Perhaps in some ways the need for in-depth preparation was eased by the internet and the proliferation of sites containing all the information and data you could possibly need.

But that has moved back in the other direction since I joined *The Athletic*. When I report on a match now, my editors don't want me just to do the nuts-and-bolts report you can read in any newspaper. They want something more thematic that our readers couldn't find anywhere else, so often my focus will be narrower and more in-depth, whether it's on a certain player, a certain tactical question, a manager etc.

And that requires more preparation than ever before. It involves a lot of research — and in many cases interviews — before I set off from home. When you're reporting on a specific issue or subject, for a well-informed (and often club-specific) audience like we have at *The Athletic*, you have to be well prepared.

What is it like to produce coverage of a game or report live from a game compared to going to a game to take it in as a fan?

Totally different. I'm pretty sure everyone who writes about football for a living started out as a fan; it's not one of those jobs you would just fall into without a prior interest in football. It's not for the casual observer.

But from the moment you go into the press box, you have to watch the game differently. You're there to do a job, usually under severe pressure to meet a deadline. You're watching two teams, not one.

There are some reporters who almost seem to abandon their allegiance the moment they receive their first press accreditation. I've always found that hard to understand, but you have to be professional, restrained and focus on your work rather than losing yourself in the moment.

There have been times (many times) when my team has scored and I've struggled to contain my joy in the press box, but we're talking about a clenched/shaken fist rather than screaming at the top of my voice and jumping up and down on my seat for the next ten minutes. If you're writing a report, you haven't got time to lose yourself — and of course you also need to try to keep a clear head rather than allow yourself to get partisan.

The way you report can change, though, depending on your role and the outlet in question. If you report exclusively on one club — particularly if you support the club in question — you can legitimately report in a way that is designed to speak to the fanbase rather than, for example, a national newspaper's entire readership. That doesn't equate to cheerleading, by the way; sometimes it can mean being much more critical.

Since I've joined *The Athletic*, I have done a lot less match-reporting in the press box and I've gone to a lot more matches as a fan. I think it's healthy for journalists to do that — not least so that we realise how bloody expensive it has become and how lucky and privileged we are.

Late goals and drama are great for fans and pundits alike. However, they can be a logistical nightmare for writers who have to change copy at fine notice approaching an editorial deadline. What does that feel like and what is the most memorable time that you can recall it happening to you?

It has happened so many times. And if we're talking about reporting on an evening match for a newspaper, the on-the-whistle report is precisely what it sounds like; it has to be submitted the moment the match finishes. Often it's the very last page to be finalised before the newspaper is printed, so you really can't hang about.

There are times where you can feel that last-minute goal coming, so even if you've got an intro and top few paragraphs sketched out, you're aware of the possibility it's going to have to be scrapped. That's fine.

The problem is when it comes from nowhere: when it goes from 0-1 to 2-1 in almost the blink of an eye. It has happened to me countless times. You just have to stay calm, even as the night editor is screaming down the phone asking where your copy is. You have to change the top one or two hundred words of your report as quickly as possible – and hope that it isn't too jarring to read when it appears in print.

The ones that I've found harder over the years are those nights when the match keeps twisting one way and then the other and you don't ever get a clear sense of how it's going to end. I remember finding it really difficult in my first year working for *The Times*, feeling the pressure to live up to a certain standard of writing when often it was a battle just to meet the deadline.

Two games that stick out from that 2000/01 season are an FA Cup tie where Tranmere Rovers came from 3-0 down to beat Southampton 4-3. It was a crazy game and, to make matters much worse, Prenton Park was (and probably still is) horrendous when it came to plug sockets, phone lines etc. There was no internet access, so I was having to try to convey this drama down the phone to bewildered copytakers in an office in Wetherby, struggling to make myself heard above the crowd. Technological advances have made life much easier, thankfully.

The other game that sticks out from that season is the UEFA Cup final between Liverpool and Alaves in Dortmund. It was the biggest match I had ever covered at that time and, again, I felt like I was under real pressure to produce something decent. It was a basket-case of a game, Liverpool eventually winning 5-4 thanks to a golden goal (actually an own goal) in extra time, and I just didn't know what to write when the game ended so abruptly. It's the closest I've come to writer's block.

It's actually harder when you're writing the 'colour piece' — the analysis/commentary that usually goes next to the match report. With these pieces, you generally have to come up with an idea and commit to it and get the whole thing written as the game is going on. Sometimes you'll be writing a piece on, for example, a player being off-colour and you'll be ruminating about his loss of form. . . and then he'll score two goals in the final few minutes and you have to change your article very, very quickly.

My favourite of these stories concerns a game which I didn't report on: the 1999 Champions League final between Manchester United and Bayern Munich. There are writers who, as the match unfolded with United trailing 1-0 and performing pretty terribly, based their entire article on how Alex Ferguson had gambled with his team selection and tactics and got it wrong (which I think was a reasonable evaluation, by the way, even if history tells a different story).

And then United, unforgettably, scored twice in the dying moments of the game, causing bedlam in the stands. . . and mayhem in the press box. It was too late to rewrite those articles; they just had got to press pretty much as they were written, save for a hastily changed into and a trite '. . . until the incredible climax' on the end. The funny thing is that when Ferguson and his players flew back from Barcelona to Manchester, the flight was full of the first editions, whose reports read more like post-mortems than

'Glory, glory Man United'. Ferguson was never slow to remind those who had evidently written him and his team off.

Last but not least, based on your career so far, what advice would you give to any aspiring football writers?

I sometimes think there's a misconception of what football journalism is. It isn't just sitting in the press box reporting on big matches or interviewing famous players. But nor should it just be about sitting in an office, trying to recycle content to meet the daunting targets set up by digital editors. There's so much emphasis on 'clickbait'. I hate it.

If you're going to become a successful journalist, you need to stand out. To stand out, you need to produce high-quality articles. Putting a clickbait headline on a press-conference quote might be considered 'content' these days, but I don't think that is a sustainable way to run an online operation or to maintain a career as a journalist.

Journalism is about stories — breaking stories, telling stories. Frankly, you need to get up off your backside — or, if you really are chained to a desk, get on the phone, make contacts, build relationships and use those relationship to try to gain information and tell your readers something they don't know.

Above all, I would urge any aspiring football writer to throw themselves into it. . . and to enjoy it. Think of all the other jobs you could be doing. Or in the cases of most of us, all the other jobs you couldn't possibly be doing. You have got the opportunity to write about football FOR A LIVING. It's a very competitive field, so give it everything you've got.

*****

Craig Burley
Punditry as it should be

After playing for Chelsea, Celtic, Derby County, Dundee, Preston North End and Walsall – and making forty-six appearances for Scotland – Craig Burley has become a football pundit, working for BBC, ESPN and BT Sport.

As a footballer, you won trophies in Scottish football and English football, as well as representing Scotland at major international tournaments. What are your personal highlights from your time as a player?

As a teenager, I dreamed of being a footballer so the highlight for me has to be the fact that I was able to become a professional player and play for as many years as I did.

I left home in Scotland for London at the age of fourteen and I battled home sickness which was tough. I needed to show resilience during those early years and that then enabled me to break into the team at Chelsea, win an FA Cup and play week in week out in the Premier League.

Playing for Celtic and winning the league title that stopped Rangers winning ten in a row while also winning Scottish Player of the Year in that season was also very special. As was playing and scoring at a World Cup with Scotland.

My career was the stuff of dreams for me and I do not look back with many regrets.

I do have some frustrations in regard to fitness because when I look back on my career now, I would do things differently in terms of taking the fitness aspect of the game much more seriously.

The reason I say that is because in the 1990s, British football was much more relaxed in its attitude towards the importance of fitness and recovery compared to the game today as sports science and nutritionists were not common at football clubs like they are today.

Despite that, I would never change the era that I played in as we had great times at the various clubs that I represented whether that was Chelsea, Scotland, Celtic or Derby. I look back on my time playing the game with real fondness.

You retired from football and moved into punditry. Was that an easy transition for you to make?

Punditry was something that I first tried in my late twenties while I was still playing. I knew a few people at BBC Scotland and Colin Davidson at Sky Sports. I did some work with them and Richard Keys on *Super Sunday* at Sky too.

Despite having those experiences while playing, I did not think that I would automatically transition from being a player into becoming a pundit.

Things sort of fell into my lap in terms of how the full-time transition happened.

A company called Setanta Sports shocked everyone by buying exclusive rights to showcase Scottish football in U.K.

They recruited Colin Davidson from Sky who I had worked with before and he called me what I was up to. I had just left Derby County at the time and I remember telling Colin that I felt frustrated with injuries and that I was not enjoying my football as much as I used to for that reason.

He replied with an old-fashioned Scottish phrase by telling me that I sounded 'scunnered' and followed that up by asking if I would be interested in working on Setanta's Scottish football coverage.

The only question I asked in response was who would I be working with? When Colin told me that it was Rob MacLean then my response was yes without any doubts.

That is how my punditry career started. I was lucky that Setanta signed Colin and that he wanted me to work for him but on the other hand, I could have sat on my arse and not bothering doing the work with Sky Sports and the BBC while I playing to get experience of the media.

So, I think it was a mixture of luck and being willing to work and learn how to improve as a broadcaster in those early years that helped me too.

The hardest thing that I found in the early months of moving into punditry was realising what side of the fence I was now on. I was no longer Craig Burley, the footballer.

I quickly had to realise that I was Craig Burley, the pundit and ensure that I did not let previous relationships from my playing days stop me from giving the honest opinion that I was being paid to give in my role.

Given that early realisation, what do you believe makes a good pundit?

Everyone has a different opinion on the answer to what makes a good pundit.

My personal view is that when you become a pundit, you need to accept that you are not being employed by football clubs but by a broadcaster who is paying you to give an honest opinion on whatever game you are covering.

You cannot say 'Oh I cannot give an opinion on that incident because player X is a pal of mine or on club Y because you used to play there.'

You are not there as a pundit to be popular. Sure, if you are popular then that is a bonus, but you are there in that role to be honest and call things as you see them.

I do not want to give easy pats on the back to those within the game because that is not the reality. You need to judge individual games, players and incidents as you see them and express that view without fear of upsetting anyone.

As long as your view is true to yourself and it is not an opinion that you are trying to say only for affect then you are doing what a pundit should in my opinion.

I never say things when I am working as a pundit for a reaction from others or for click bait.

I may have made the odd mistake on that part over the years but on the whole, I do not call games with any preconceived ideas.

I am not in the role to be given pats on the back by old clubs etc. I am there to give an honest view on the game or a player or an incident within the game that I can back up.

Punditry should be about honesty and being forthright with your view rather than simply telling people what you think that they want to hear.

You experienced a unique scenario early in your punditry career where your Uncle George Burley was Scotland manager during a tough time for the national team and you were a pundit calling those games. Did such a delicate situation of calling games involving a close family member ever test your resolve in your beliefs about punditry?

It did not make things harder for me because, although I believe that forthright honesty is the imperative in your role as a pundit, it should never involve a needless character assassination of a person.

There is never any need to make punditry personal. It is simply a matter of calling things as you see them.

George was in charge of Scotland during a tough spell and I had to call that for what it was. He knew that as manager of Scotland, he needed results and he also knew that I had to do my job of being honest about what I was watching.

You cannot lie to the viewer at home. They can see through that right away. I approached George's games with the same manner that I would for any other manager in the game.

I know that it is fashionable now to support football teams as pundits and nail your colours to the mast. That personally is not my approach and does not sit too well with me, but I understand it and that things evolve and over time and working in TV is no different to that,

*****

James Rowe
From football fan to multilinguistic reporter and interviewer

James Rowe is a football writer and Dutch football expert. His articles have featured in World of Football Index and he has appeared on talkSPORT and Love Sport Radio.

You have been on a remarkable journey to go from a passionate football fan to becoming a British football writer and Dutch football expert living in the Netherlands. How would you sum up that rollercoaster of a journey?

It has indeed been a rollercoaster of a journey for me as I left the UK in my early twenties to relocate to the Netherlands. However, in the words of my mother, it has been the greatest decision that I have ever made. I am exceptionally proud of what I have achieved since relocating to Amsterdam.

It all started thanks to my football club: Arsenal.

I can honestly say that my football club changed my life as without Arsenal, I probably would never have swapped the UK for the Netherlands. I travelled to Amsterdam as a tourist for the first time in 2003 at the age of nineteen to watch Arsenal face Ajax in the second group phase of the Champions League.

I was immediately charmed by the city of Amsterdam, and I knew that from my first few hours of travelling around the city that I wanted my future to be here. I had always dreamed of living and working abroad when a young child and my mind was made up when I returned home after my four-day trip.

I told my mother upon arrival that I believed that I had seen the future for myself and that it would be living and working in Amsterdam. She laughed and reminded me that I have only returned home a few hours ago and to think carefully about what I was saying.

I then started to save up money to make my dream a reality and my mother could then understand that I was serious. She supported me the whole way and just two years after that Ajax-Arsenal match that I had attended in 2003, I was off to the Netherlands to start a new life for myself.

Even when I had packed my belongings and was preparing to set off on my journey to the Netherlands, I remember family members and friends thinking that I was joking when I said that I was going to relocate mainly because my experience of a foreign away day with my club Arsenal was the main factor and motivation for my move.

However, I made the move and I am still living and working in the city until this day. I love living here and I am fluent in Dutch, I am fortunate to be able to watch Ajax first hand on a regular basis and interview professional players and managers from the Netherlands in their mother tongue.

You have interviewed hundreds of professional players and managers from across the globe. Your passion for languages has assisted you along the way to interview players and managers in their mother tongue in Dutch, Spanish, Portuguese and English. What are the realities of being a multi-linguistic writer and how much work is involved in the translation process?

First and foremost, it is a privilege. It sometimes feels like having a special superpower when you are able to do something that not many people are able to do.

My journey into football writing started when I became a

translator for the Dutch football website 'Football Oranje'. I would translate pre and post-match interviews from Dutch into English with the likes of Matthias De Ligt, Frenkie De Jong and many others.

After doing this for eighteen months, I started to think that I could do this myself, surely. I approached various clubs with a view to speaking to a player or a staff member that they were employing at the time.

Early in my journey, I believe that curiosity was the key to me being granted interviews by clubs because it is not every day that a British football writer approaches a Dutch player or manager with the view to conducting an interview in Dutch.

Wiljan Vloet and FC Den Bosch granted me my first interview in the summer of 2016. I was invited to the stadium and we spoke for an hour in view of the pitch about his time as a manager at clubs such as ADO Den Haag, Sparta Rotterdam and his involvement with FC Den Bosch.

He also talked to me about his time managing in the Greek Super League with Niki Volos and admitted to me that he struggled to succeed there due to his inability to speak Greek and the communication barrier that was created as a result.

His message in that interview can be translated to football writing as when conducting an interview with a footballing personality, it is vital that they understand what you are asking and that you understand clearly what it is that they are communicating to you as the interviewer.

Following that interview, I continued to interview an array of Dutch footballing personalities and gradually gathered momentum as a writer and interviewer which led to me being approached by World Football Index. From there, I have gone on to conduct over four hundred interviews with professional players and managers from all levels of the world game.

My portfolio includes interviews with European Cup winners Jamie Carragher and Viv Anderson as well as highly regarded managers such as Graham Potter and Danny Cowley among many others.

I am very proud of all that I have achieved so far and arguably my biggest compliment came from former Manchester United, Barcelona and current Netherland's coach Frans Hoek. After I interviewed him in 2020, he complimented my understanding and fluency of the Dutch language and my thorough preparation for our interview.

That meant everything to me because I prepare thoroughly for every interview regardless of the stature and standing of the player or manager in question and I work meticulously on the translation from Dutch to English to make sure that every single piece that I produce is the best that it can possibly be.

The process can take a couple of hours in total, but it is a joy and not a chore foe me. I know how lucky I am to be able to speak to those within the game of football and I do not take any interview for granted.

Based on your experience of writing and interviewing people of all standings within football, what do you believe are the secrets to a top interview?

The two main secrets to conducting a successful interview in my opinion are the rhythm of the interview and listening.

Firstly, some footballers are more talkative than others and it is important that you allow them to feel comfortable by speaking to them at a pace that works for them. I believe that is important to emphasise that you are interested in their journey in football rather than looking for a sensational quote to create a headline.

Secondly, listening is vital. You may have prepared a structure for an interview, but you should never be afraid to follow the natural flow of an anecdote within an interview. For example, I was fortunate to speak to former England footballer Terry Fenwick who opened up on the 1986 World Cup campaign in great detail. I gave him the time and space to tell me about all of his experiences in a relaxed manner which led to that interview being one of my most well received.

His tales of facing Diego Maradona and the impact of Sir Bobby Robson were particularly enthralling. He told me that before the World Cup quarter final between England and Maradona, Sir Bobby told him and the England team not to worry about Diego as he 'only had one foot anyway.' The comment was delivered in jest and Sir Bobby had a huge grin on his face as he delivered it.

Terry said that the comment helped relax the squad before the game but within minutes, the task of facing Maradona was no longer a joke. He was twisting and turning Terry and his England teammates inside out. So much so that Terry tried to kick him to put a stop to him. Unfortunately for him and England, it was to no avail as after a couple of minutes at the side of the pitch, Diego marched back onto the field and took complete control of the game to end England's hopes.

That is only one example of numerous anecdotes that have been shared with me. Listening attentively during such time is key because to gain insight like this, you have to take the information in and ask the correct follow up question when it is appropriate to do so.

CHAPTER SIX
The art of football commentary

Martin Tyler
The voice of football commentary

A journalist since the 1960s, Martin Tyler is best known as the Sky Sports commentator. In April 2003, Tyler was voted as the Premier League Commentator of the Decade.

He has covered all the major tournaments, including the Champions League and the World Cup.

You've commentated on iconic moments in world football for decades including finals of the Champions League and various international tournaments. You have also been synonymous with historic stand-alone moments like the Aguero goal in 2012. Do you prepare for a big moment in any way or does your reaction come naturally to you in the moment?

It's a natural thing. I don't think you can prepare for the unpredictable. I also don't think that anyone in their right mind could have predicted the situation that Manchester City found themselves going into during injury time back in 2012.

You prepare in many ways by ensuring that you know the facts and figures of the fixture and cover all bases that the game could go in to be across all of the different angles. However, the big moments in matches are spontaneous on the field and on commentary too.

In most cases, you won't use many of the facts that you have prepared because all of us as commentators over prepare.

I have been asked over the years to recreate the Aguero commentary and other famous moments, but you can't. It is something that can only happen in the moment and that you are taken to by the drama of that occasion and the time in question.

It is special to be in those moments because nothing is better than watching history unfold before your eyes.

Managers and players have talked about tweaking their preparation for cup finals or one-off occasions in the past. Are those occasions business as usual for you or can you feel any added pressure like the players and staff on the pitch feel?

It is business as usual. The most important game as a commentator is always the next one whether it's a pre-season friendly, a youth cup game or a major cup final. I've commentated on many of each of those throughout the years and I always ensure that my full focus is on the next commentary regardless of the game. You cannot underestimate any game because you know what is expected of you as a commentator.

I learned to think about my role in different ways quite recently when in accompanied a group of students whom I mentor on a visit to the McLaren F1 team. One of the students asked how much freedom does the driver of an F1 car have and how much is down to the preparation and tactics of team?

It was a question that made me think of my role. It was a good analogy for me to think about what percentage of what I do is pre-planned preparation and how much do I leave to the freedom of the day itself.

I am not even entirely sure of how that would equate for me. I imagine that it varies from game to game.

However, it has to be a mixture of preparation in advance but always be prepared to watch what is really happening in the moment and respond to it without being restricted by any preconceived ideas of how a game might turn out based on your research.

Commentary is a reactive job. For example, you may think that a team will play a particular formation and after the first five minutes of a game, it is clear that they are not. You have to adapt and call what is happening at any given time even if it sounds like you're contradicting yourself.

How important is it as a lead commentator to develop chemistry and a shared understanding with your co-commentary partner?

I'll be honest with you, I'm usually so much older than my co-commentator, that I feel like it is my responsibility to ensure that I do all that I can to make sure that I can make their broadcast experience as comfortable as possible.

The co-commentator is normally a stronger listen for a viewer because they have been out on the pitch and played the game at the level that they are commentating on whereas my experience stopped at the Isthmian League. Although, I have coached at National League level with Woking and Dartford which is a higher level than I ever thought that I would reach.

I always want to make sure that any co-commentator is comfortable and has all of the information that they want.

We very rarely revisit the game after the occasion. If they are happy at the end of the broadcast then I am happy although I am never happy with myself and my own performance. That's the way commentary is. You are always striving for a level of perfection that doesn't exist although that doesn't stop you striving for it.

You referenced the age of many of your co-commentators. How does it make you feel when you start working with a former player for the first time who you have commentated on during the highs and lows of their career?

It is an honour and privilege to be able to dip into their experiences having been at some of those games too. It is fascinating to find out more about them.

Part of the reason that I enjoy being involved is the fact that I wanted to be a professional footballer but never made the grade whereas these guys have been there and done it. They continued on the journey that I set out on and so I admire them so much for what they have achieved.

I look at it with affection and it is nice to have the privilege of talking football on the air and off it with people who have been at the top of the tree in the game as both players and managers.

You are the voice of the Premier League for so many. You have been the lead commentator on the English game for the entirety of my lifetime. The league began in 1992, could you have ever anticipated the rise of the league from where it was in the beginning to the global juggernaut that it is today?

No, the only thing about it is that I always felt the love and affection for football long before the Premier League as I'm sure does everyone who watched football before that era.

Then, the Premier League started and the draw was irresistible for me. I am glad that so many more people have found it as the league has grown.

The way that the game is run now has attracted so many people to it. Whether I could have anticipated it, I don't know but I could have told you in 1992 that football is a great game, a global game that deserves a large audience and I would say the same today.

Television is far more accessible across the globe which has helped and the medium of broadcasting is incredible to be able to take the pictures from a small vicinity of a football ground and take it around the world.

I've always found that fascinating. I remember broadcasting from Copacabana beach at the World Cup in 2014 and thinking how can I be standing here and my kids are watching at home in England?

The rise of technology within television has been remarkable and has complemented the rise of Premier League football too.

Based on your career in broadcasting that has spanned decades working at the highest level, what do you believe has been the key to your longevity in such a competitive industry?

I'm always a bit surprised that things have happened as they have. I don't remember saying it, but I was told that I said early in my commentary career that success would be to be still be doing the job in twenty years' time.

I've been doing it over forty years later and it all comes back to the love of the game of football. I am never bored watching football whether I am broadcasting or not.

I love the intrigue of how one team will try and set up to combat another and the fact that the game itself is gripping.

Added to that, I always love the people who play the game itself and have the skills to entertain the world. My passion for the game has never gone and if it ever did then people wouldn't want me to commentate on it and I wouldn't want to commentate on it anymore either.

However, I do not see that happening anytime soon because when you have the team news and the ball is on the centre spot, there is a buzz that I and many others feel which doesn't go away.

I was not a trained broadcaster. I watched what the football was and went from an avid viewer, a would-be player and a fan who got the chance to find a different way of fulfilling my dream of being involved in football.

It has been a football life and I hope that there is more to come as well. I feel so lucky to have had this opportunity. I have worked hard but many people work hard so I can't say that is a special gift of mine.

The fact that football has never bored me or been a chore has been the key. I am always on the edge of my seat and I'll carry that with me to the end. I would never want to look back and change any of it.

*****

Alan Smith
The key to co-commentary

Beginning his career with non-league Alvechurch, Alan Smith joined Leicester City in 1982, forming a prolific strike partnership with Gary Lineker.

In 1987, Smith joined Arsenal where he spent the rest of his career, winning two First Division titles, one FA Cup, one League Cup, one Charity Shield and one European Cup Winners' Cup.

You made the transition from top level footballer to co-commentary with Sky. How did you manage that transition and was broadcasting always an avenue that you wanted to explore?

No, it did not occur to me that I would become a broadcaster because I always wanted to have a go at writing. I studied languages at university and I had a decent education so I thought that might be niche for me because not many – if any – former footballers wrote themselves.

I would never have dreamed in a million years that I would be doing it for the next twenty-five years because I honestly did not think that my character was suited to it.

I am quite a reserved person, not an extrovert in any way. However, it started for me towards the end of my playing career when I was asked to go a couple of things for Sky while I was injured.

I started as a pundit in the studio for Arsenal games at that time and I continued that when I retired along with a role with *Soccer Saturday*. From there, I was asked to go into co-commentary which I've been doing ever since. It goes to show that you just never know how things are going to turn out.

I've worked hard over the years and always prepared thoroughly for each game like it is my first. Maybe that is why I have lasted so long.

Can you talk me through your preparation ahead of a co-commentary?

Lead commentators are much different to co-comms because we don't need to do as much preparation in comparison.

We get a statistics pack send to us by our stats team at Sky about both teams that are set to face each other. I always started by looking through that then by going back and watching previous matches of both sides on video.

I then like to read the local papers of both sides to analyse what is being said and gauge the mood around each club and find out who might be injured. I always want to have a flavour of the occasion before going in to it.

Much like playing, it is during the match itself, that your work counts. Your role as a co-commentator is to add something to the pictures for the viewer. Think before you speak.

If you do not have anything useful to say then the best thing to do is keep your mouth shut. I've always gone by that because it's easy to waffle away just to say something. Giving insight and a player's perspective of a situation is my main role and that's what I aim for in every broadcast.

You have worked with Martin Tyler for many years covering Premier League football on Sky. How important is it to you to build a strong relationship with the lead commentator?

It's important and comes naturally by working together. The more you work together then the more you know their individual habits and how to gauge when they will stop and when you can come in to speak.

It only comes with practice, but every lead commentator is different.

Rob Hawthorne and Bill Leslie are our other two lead commentators at Sky and they both have different characteristics from Martin and from one another.

I have to say that working with Martin is a such a joy. He is a legend of the commentary world. I can click on a game from 1979 on YouTube and there he is commentating on it. It's ridiculous. His dedication to his craft is there for all to see.

I have learned so much from him over the years. He absolutely loves football and what he does which helps me. His attention to detail is second to none and that is why he is still at the top of his game to this day.

As a lover of football, what is the biggest joy that co-commentary gives you?

The biggest joy is when there is a big moment in a game such as a great goal and you watch back and think that you have done it justice.You have to careful not to simply repeat what the commentator has just said. You want to add something different which is not always easy.

I always think back to Wayne Rooney's overhead kick in the Manchester derby. Martin had summed the goal up brilliantly and I was sitting there thinking what else I could add as the replays as rolling. I was pleased with how that went.

Sometimes you are unhappy because you look back and worry that you were a bit flat because sometimes if you start like that then it can be part to pick it up. Thankfully, that has not happened too often.

You are always at the mercy of the game and if there is not a lot happening then there is not a lot you can do about that. The exciting games with lots of goals take care of themselves. They are easy to commentate on because there is so much to talk about and be enthused by.

How do you evaluate your performance as a co-commentator? Do you watch your games back or judge it based on how you feel at the end of a broadcast?

You know how a game has gone but even now, I do try and watch back although not for the entire match. Not as much as I should do probably because I don't like listening back to my own work.

There is always a three-minute edit available or you can listen to more of the game.

I like to make sure that I am not guilty of repeating the same phrase over and over again. Only by listening back can you correct that because people don't always tend to tell you if you are.

Finally, Alan, you and Martin Tyler were lead commentators on the popular video game franchise FIFA for many years. How did commentating for a video game compare to working on a live match?

The main difference is that you do not have any pictures in front of you to commentate on. It's all in your mind. It's your imagination that is required. We are given a thick wad of scenarios and told what kind of scene to describe in our own words in five or six different ways so that it can remain relatively fresh on the game over time.

A good vocabulary is key for that as is thinking in your feet. It is very time consuming because you are in a sound booth recording for around three or four hours at a time. You can feel frazzled after it, but it was a great thing to be able to do. Martin and I loved doing the work for the game.

We would record together and having each other to bounce off made it feel more natural even though it was not on the gantry like we are used to.

*****

Jock Brown
Commentating on clubs, countries and Craig

Brother of former Scotland and Aberdeen manager Craig, Jock Brown was a solicitor by profession and is also a broadcaster, commentating for BBC Scotland, Sky Sports, Setanta Sports and others.

You have had the honour of commentating on historic finals in Scottish football over the years. How do you prepare for such occasions to try and capture the big moments in the right tone?

I commentated on cup finals and international matches between 1978 and 1997. In those days I had to carry out all my own research, which I did by completing copious notes manually every week. Sadly, the internet was not available for most of that time. Similarly, there were no researchers made available to me by STV or the BBC. That became routine while working for Sky, when a detailed portfolio of information would be prepared for you.

Before any match, including cup finals, I prepared a chart showing the names of all the players, and personal details relating to each one – age, background, transfer fees paid, goals scored, penalties taken, red and yellow cards received, and any relationships with opponents. These were colour coded and studied before every match, because it is notoriously difficult to refer to notes during the match.

For big occasions I always like to have a period of silent contemplation for about half an hour before the game. By that time the homework should have been committed to memory. So this period is important in preparing mentally and psychologically for a very long period of unscripted commentary. During that period also, I can become immersed in the atmosphere in the stadium, so that I am ready for my voice to blend into these surroundings.

I also remind myself of the fact that I really don't need to work my voice as hard as I might have to in a half-empty stadium.

The other key thing I always reminded myself about was

the fact that I must not get carried away by the occasion. It was essential to remain calm and focused – even more so in a big match. With huge crowd involvement it is also appropriate to say a little less than usual, strangely enough.

In summary, the preparation for a big match like a cup final is principally mental and psychological. It is vital to remain calm (although you may not act as though you are calm!) because you are aware that choosing the right words over key incidents in a big match is crucial. You will have a lifetime to regret screwing it up!

It is also important to remain conscious of the fact that you are giving a performance which you hope will enhance the occasion.

Your brother Craig is a high-profile personality within football having managed Scotland and historic football clubs such as Preston North End and Motherwell. Did you find it tricky to commentate and analyse him and his teams during your career?

I never found it difficult to commentate on matches where Craig was managing one of the participating teams. The vast majority of such matches involved Scotland, so I was much more concerned about the issues described in answer one than the fact that he was managing.

There was one particular match where the issue was raised about him being in charge of Scotland. That was the Estonia v Scotland match in Monaco after the famous 'no-show' by Estonia in Tallin.

Scotland played very poorly in a nil-nil draw. I then had to interview Craig after the match. I remember being upset when the director told me through my earpiece that I had to forget he was my brother and ask the appropriate tough questions. Such an instruction was completely unnecessary. Indeed, I was given praise afterwards for 'putting him through the ringer' in the interview. I wasn't happy about that either. I just did my job, as I saw it, professionally.

No one appreciated that more than Craig. I spoke to him at the airport on the way home and pointed out that I had to make the interview appropriate and real. He was completely untroubled and said he hadn't noticed either way – he was much more concerned about the performance and the result.

What advice would you give to any budding commentator who aspires to a career in radio or television?

My advice to a radio commentator would be to remain conscious at all times that the listener can't see anything. Accordingly, he/she should keep telling him/her where the ball is. The basic idea is to try to describe the action in a way whereby the listener can see the game in his mind's eye. So get a tape of the late old maestro David Francey in the 1960s and 1970s!

My advice to a budding television commentator would be to remember that the star of the broadcast is the picture, not the commentator. The role of the commentator is to enhance the viewer's understanding and appreciation of the action. You do that first by identifying the players, then by providing the insight which is available to someone watching the match live as against on a restricted television screen.

Basically a television commentator should scarcely be noticed – his words should just have entered your psyche to enhance your understanding and appreciation as you watch the game. A commentator is similar to a referee – if he hasn't been noticed the chances are he has done a great job.

CHAPTER SEVEN
Anchoring the game

Jeff Stelling
Mr Saturday Afternoon

Jeff Stelling is best known as the presenter of *Gillette Soccer Saturday* for Sky Sports. He has also presented *Countdown* and *Alphabetical*.

You worked on *Soccer Saturday* for three decades on which was an incredibly popular show. In terms of the preparation of that show, where does it start for you because when you're on air, you always seem to have a real range of knowledge of local opinion and national opinion?

Yeah well, it's a classic cliche isn't it you know, it's like the forth bridge used to be when you finished one part you started another. So, it's case of preparing all week for one show then starting all over again for the next.

It did not used to be like that, to be honest. I used to think it was okay to turn up on a Friday, early afternoon and do all my prep then. It is pretty much never ending. It starts with the basics of trying to watch as much live football as you can and watching *Match of the Day*. Watching football league highlights. Then, during the week, reading as many newspapers as possible and websites, occasionally podcasts. As much as you possibly can.

Of course, on top of that there are the ever-changing stats which, generally speaking, take a couple of full-on days to compile. It is safe to say the preparation is relentless (laughs).

In terms of the broadcast itself, you've always had great chemistry with other pundits, whether that be Rodney Marsh or George Best from years gone by to the modern day pundits like: Matt Le Tissier, Phil Thompson, Charlie Nicholas and Paul Merson.

How important is developing chemistry for a live broadcast of six hours in length?

It is crucial. It is impossible to emphasise just how important it is. Over the years, the guys I've worked with haven't just been colleagues, they've been friends. Even in my last couple of years, when the panel would change regularly between shows, I still felt that the chemistry was there as relationships grow over time.

What is unique is that the panel is made up of highly regarded current or former professionals, who can actually be daunted by appearing on live television initially.

Therefore, it is really important to me that the people who I work with on the panel feel as comfortable and as natural as possible when in front of the camera so that their natural warmth shines through to the viewers at home.

You mentioned that you worked closely with George Best who was one of the most famous footballers of all time both on and off the field. What was he really like to work with?

George was not necessarily the man the public thought he was. In the sense that he was a very gentle and quiet man. As a footballer on the pitch, he was brilliant, outgoing and flash. However, as a man, there was none of that. He was a man who had fame thrust upon him from a young age and sometimes he found it a bit difficult to cope with that fame.

I have been on nights out with George, and he would be swamped by people wanting photos and autographs, especially women. That was the case no matter who he was with. I felt for him in that regard because he was a genuinely lovely guy who would do anything for anyone. However, his situation was difficult. Fame at that level must be incredibly difficult to deal with.

I must ask you about another character who shared the panel with you, Phil Thompson. You are both known for being very

passionate and as a result you both could have heated debates on air. How much did you enjoy being able to debate with him and wind him up on air?

Phil is one of my closest friends so much so that I would trust him with my life. However, sometimes if someone says something that you disagree with, you must challenge them on it because there is no point of having a six-hour show where everyone just smiles, agrees, and nods at each other. Often, I would disagree with him because he is very opinionated as am I. Sometimes, I would conveniently disagree with him to provoke a reaction from him. His passion always showed through during these moments.

The great thing about Tommo and all the pundits that I worked with, no matter how passionately we disagreed about something, when the debate was over it was forgotten about, and we moved on. The main thing that we wanted to do was share our opinions about the game we all love and most importantly have fun and go for a beer after the show. That was the way it always was.

In terms of the show itself, were you ever shocked by the success of the show given the premise of it is five pundits watching football that the viewer cannot see at home and talking about it for hours on end?

Interestingly, that is something that when you think about it is true and could be seen as confusing to people who do not follow football.

I like to think of the show as more than a football programme. There are shows on television whether that be *Loose Women* or *Politics Today* where four or five panellists sit around talking the issues of the day and that is exactly what *Soccer Saturday* is to football fans.

That being said, I absolutely was surprised by the success of the show. It was a gradual thing, and the audience was built up slowly in the early years, but it was unlike anything else on television at the time which I think was the appeal initially for fans to give us a chance.

Over the years, various television channels have tried to copy what we did at *Soccer Saturday* which is the ultimate compliment really.

Newspapers have referred to the show as a cult hit over the years which is also great because cult tv shows tend to be popular and evoke positive memories.

What stands the show in good stead is the fact that it has stood the test of time over the last three decades even with more and more football being readily available on TV and when ITV, BBC and BT sport produced their own versions of the show in some regard.

It is my opinion that as long as there is football played on a Saturday at 3pm then there is no reason why it shouldn't carry on and flourish.

In terms of the show when you are live, Jeff, the level of precision whether it be with statistics or bringing us multiple scores at the same time from the vidiprinter. It is exhausting to watch at times as a viewer never mind what it must be like as the anchor of the show, how do you keep up with it all?

It is years of being in that position. A good comparison would be learning how to drive. When you start learning to drive you think you will never fully master the coordination of clutch, brake, acceleration, and gear changes. However, over time it becomes second nature, and you wonder how you ever struggled with that. It is all very similar. At first it seems extremely difficult, and it still does at times. You are battling with the relative importance of different games and different goals. As well as what should come first and what you might have to leave out because you have got a flood of goals coming in at the same time.

The producer sometimes might have different ideas to mine. It is very much a juggling act. However it is a juggling act which I've got used to over the years.

The biggest issues are when the vidiprinter breaks. That is the equivalent of a juggler dropping all of his balls. It makes what you are doing impossible. Difficulties with receiving pictures from different stadiums can be awkward as well. However, the vidiprinter going down is without a doubt the most difficult thing to deal with. It makes me shudder thinking about it (laughs).

Over your three decades on the show, what are your three favourite memories?

Jimmy Glass would be one of them that is for sure. That was from the days when we were a cult show as the media liked to call it. In that moment, he got a fair amount of media coverage as did we. I did a lot of homework on what could happen that day. I remember seeing Scarborough fans sitting on the pitch just waiting for the full-time score from Carlisle to come in, knowing that as it stood, they had done enough to stay up.

Carlisle had got rid of a couple of goalkeepers but due to injury they were short on numbers. They received special dispensation from the league to bring Jimmy Glass in on an emergency loan. I was very against that because they as a club had made the decision to get rid of their goalkeeper. Do not get me wrong, for an emergency loan goalkeeper to score an injury time goal that keeps a team in the football league, well that is nothing short of extraordinary even by football standards.

It is safe to say, that was a great moment that so many people remember fondly. Especially if you're not a Scarborough fan.

Of course, the Aguero goal that won Manchester City their first Premier League title in 2012 was another unbelievable moment. Of course, everyone remembers Martin Tyler's commentary, but I was unique in that I saw it from a different perspective as Paul Merson was covering the game for us live in the studio that day. We were cutting backwards and forwards between the Manchester United game and the Manchester City game because either of those sides could have won the league that day.

The United game finished, and City trailed 2-1 to QPR at home so we all thought that the title was heading the way of Sir Alex and Manchester United.

Then, City get a goal back to make it 2-2 before Aguero scores with the last kick of the ball in the City game to snatch the title from Manchester United in the most dramatic fashion.

Paul Merson's description of the action that day was just as iconic as Martin Tyler's in many ways because he captured the pure emotion behind it all. I remember him screaming at the top of his voice as the players celebrated the goal that 'they are piling on top of each other, and they will no doubt be giving each other love bites and everything!'

It was a classic moment and Paul Merson captured it perfectly as only he could. He was a joy to work with throughout the years

Other moments that stand to mind are the Watford vs Leicester play-off game in which Leicester miss a penalty that would take them to the Premier League only for Watford to go straight down the other end and score the goal that would take them into the Premier League.

Johnny Phillips covered that game for us, and he lost his voice in the midst of the live report he was giving us. It was remarkable and a moment that I will always remember.

However, the third moment that I have to pick is the famous moment from Kammy at Fratton Park when he missed the red card for Portsmouth's Anthony Vanden Borre.

That sort of moment could only happen to Kammy and only he could handle it so well as he did with great humour. That moment went viral all over the world and is mentioned to me every single day by someone who I meet whether that be in the street or in the supermarket or at a Hartlepool game.

Finally, Jeff, you left Soccer Saturday *in 2023 after three decades anchoring the show. You have watched a lot of football over the years in that role and as a Hartlepool United fan. How do you see footballing evolving in the years ahead?*

There have been so many changes over my time working on *Soccer Saturday* and my time following football as a whole.

From the back pass rule to the Bosman ruling, goal line technology and VAR being introduced. There have been many changes to football in my lifetime and not all of them have been for the better, in my opinion.

When I first started to watch football, it was incredibly rare to see a women or families in the crowd at matches. Whereas it is now common place for women, girls and families to attend matches and enjoy the game from grassroots level right through to the elite levels of the game and that is a massive positive over my lifetime.

I desperately hope that football does not succumb to a European or World super league in the future because I do not want to see such manufactured, money-oriented type of football that detaches the foundation of football as we know it.

Fans are the lifeblood of football across all levels and they should always be able to follow their team, and a super league would take that away from so many with games being staged all over the globe on a regular basis.

I hope that the ninety-two clubs in the professional leagues in England and the forty-two clubs in the professional leagues in Scotland and all the clubs down to grassroots can continue to flourish because a progressive football pyramid is what makes our game in the UK very unique.

My favourite thing about following Hartlepool did the interaction that fans can have with their heroes. I think a lot of fans of lower league clubs would say the same.

As much as I love the Premier League and the Champions League, it is a shame that fans rarely have the chance to connect with players on a human level and vice versa. Whereas, for a fan of Hartlepool or Stenhousemuir or whichever lower league team it might be, you can speak to the players by waiting on them at the team bus or by going into the supporters' club after a game.

You are so connected to the game at the lower league level and long term I would also like to see that element return to the top teams if that is at all possible with the rise of social media and attendances and all that comes with that.

Aside from that, I just want football to continue to entertain because that is what the name of the game is.

Of course, you want your team to win but football is first and foremost about enjoyment. That is how we all fell in love with the game in the first place and I hope that we never forget that feeling because football is a beautiful game in so many senses and long may it continue.

*****

Mark Pougatch
Anchoring major tournaments and working with high profile pundits

London born Mark Pougatch began his broadcasting career at

the BBC. In 1994, he became the presenter of 5 *live Sport*. In 2015, Pougatch became the main football presenter on ITV and later BT Sport. He has covered many major events including, the Champions League, Europa League and the European Championships.

You have anchoring live coverage of major tournaments for ITV in both football and rugby. How do you approach broadcasts like this that will be watched by millions of viewers live?

I prepare in the same way as I would for any broadcast, whatever the size of the audience.

Every broadcast requires the same meticulous level of preparation, the same level of work, the same level of attention and the same of respect. That is what the job demands at all times, and it is the minimum requirement of any presenter whether it be the first round of the FA Cup or a record TV audience for a single channel in this country as the Euro 2020 semi-final against Denmark was.

During such tournaments, you also work with numerous high-profile sportsmen and woman such as Roy Keane, Patrick Vieira and Emma Hayes among others. How do you manage a broadcast with high-profile personalities and ensure that each of them is able to have ample air time to have their say on the game being covered?

Graham Norton summed it up very well by stating that as presenters, it is our job to be in essence a waiter. We present our guests to you as the watching public in the best possible way.

I approach each broadcast by talking to all of the pundits beforehand so that they know the areas we are going to cover, and in order to get a sense of what they feel about a certain topic. After that I can hear and gauge if someone is not as involved or has not as much as the others. It is not an exact science. Time pressures like advert breaks come into play but it is my responsibility as a host to make sure that everyone has had a chance to shine across the duration of any broadcast.

Sportsmen and woman across all sports have their performances analysed by fans and pundits alike. As a television presenter, how do you evaluate and analyse your own performance as a broadcaster?

I'm very self critical and always ensure that evaluate what I have done and what I could have done better, but I also have some very trusted people in the industry who will always give me honest, critical feedback.

It is no good looking for people to constantly blow smoke up your backside; you will not maintain the necessary standards that way. I tend to reflect personally and speak to a selected few people involved in the broadcast itself and gauge the reaction of the viewing public. That way I know that I will receive me the honest appraisal I need.

*****

Dan Thomas
Broadcasting worldwide

Dan Thomas spent five years working for Real Madrid TV before joining ESPN as a studio host and commentator. He has covered matches in the Champions League and La Liga, amongst others.

You worked at Real Madrid for many years before moving to the US to work for ESPN on their global football show ESPN FC. What are the similarities and differences between working for a major club like Real Madrid and a major broadcaster in ESPN?

Inevitably, when you work for a club channel, you have to tow the party line at least to some extent.

You need to always remain conscious as to who your audience is and who is paying your wages. In that sense, I wouldn't be as critical as I would be in my role at ESPN.

At ESPN, we have much wider scope to what we can discuss compared to working at a club because you are covering the game across different leagues from numerous angles rather than through the prism of one club and one angle.

ESPN FC is broadcast in over a hundred territories around the globe. You usually work alongside three or four pundits per show. How important is it as an anchor to develop a strong rapport with each pundit?

Strong chemistry is vital and has absolutely been the key to the success of the show. I have learned over the years which subjects are better to suited to which pundits in order to ensure that each show flows well.

The fluency of the show needs to be strong and you never want to put a pundit into a position where they are talking about something that they do not know too much about. If that happens then the audience spots it straight away and doesn't make for a good show.

The camaraderie that I have with our pundits such as Gab Marcotti, Steve Nicol, Craig Burley and Julien Laurens is one of the key factors in the success of *ESPN FC*.

Confrontation among pundits is inevitable given their passion and differing experiences as players and coaches. What is the best way to you deal with strong debate between pundits?

Again, chemistry and trust is key.

My role during any heated debate is to sit back and allow it to simmer by saying nothing but also to know when to step in when to move the discussion on.

As crazy as it may sound, sometimes saying nothing as a host is the most effective thing that you can do at key points during a broadcast.

You invite questions from the general public on ESPN FC for your pundits. Do you read these in advance or do you see them at the same time as the pundits live on air?

I see them at the same time as the pundits. The producer of the show chooses the questions and I literally see them when the segment begins.

Fans of the show enjoy the viewers questions because of the unpredictability of it. The pundits genuinely do not know what they are going to be asked and sometimes the questions aren't even football related.

They usually get asked about the old stories from their playing days which tends to be popular with viewers. Steve Nicol always comes to fore during these segments because you never quite know what he is going to say.

How did you handle lockdown during the coronavirus pandemic in 2020 when you continued to broadcast the show from home but weren't in the same room as anyone else working on the show?

It took a little bit of time to get used to, particularly the delay that is common when you are broadcasting from various locations at once because our pundits were all based at home too.

I missed watching the games that we would be covering with our team because that is one of the highlights with my role.

Former footballers see the game differently to you or I. They have an eye for things that we often don't notice.

Finally, Dan, you have interviewed numerous high-profile footballers including the great Pele. I believe that your chat with him did not quite go to plan. What happened?

Those type of interviews are always exciting because you are speaking to an expert in football and someone who is a legend of football, sport or film.

Usain Bolt was a highlight of mine in terms of an interviewee. He came into our studio and he was a fan of the show. He is also a big Manchester United fan so he knew his football which helps massively because I've interviewed Sir Lewis Hamilton and Hugh Jackman before and their football knowledge was not the strongest so you need to try and talk about other things.

Whereas Bolt was really cool to be able to speak because he is the fastest man on earth and one of the greatest Olympians of all time. That was my favourite interview without a doubt.

However, the Pele interview was an absolute disaster.

First of all, his English is not the greatest. Remember it is not his first language so that is understandable.

He had just arrived in New York ahead of the Super Bowl where he would be watching the game as part of a corporate sponsorship that he had with Subway at the time.

We spoke about football and his career and things were going well so I thought to myself that it would be a great time to ask him about the Super Bowl for the last question.

Because he was going to the event, I assumed he would have a favourite team or an opinion on it. I asked him who he thought would win the Super Bowl and he looked at me blankly because he has no idea what I was talking about.

Then, rather than moving on, like an idiot I doubled down and asked him again just in case he hadn't understood the question. Why I did that, I will never know because again, he had no clue and we had reached the end of our time, so we had a rushed goodbye afterwards as well.

So, please take my advice and if you are ever interviewing Pele, do not ask him about the Super Bowl!

Gerard McDade
The reality of anchoring club television

Gerard McDade is author of *Celtic – The Supersonic '70s* and co-wrote *The Last* Line with Packie Bonner and *His Name is McNamara* with Jackie McNamara. McDade has also worked for Celtic, BBC and TALK107, and he has contributed to multiple newspapers and magazines.

You have worked for Celtic Football Club and Greenock Morton as part of the club media and in house commentary team. What is it like to work directly for a football club and be tasked with producing engaging content?

For someone who enjoys the game and, especially the history of it, working directly for a club is always an interesting experience. One of the joys is travelling to away games, perhaps in Europe – Kazakhstan was quite a gig – or even through to East Fife, as it affords one the chance to take in the history of the club.

In order – my job at Celtic was to produce and present for the club channel, CelticTV, write articles, organise matchday and provide commentary. Yes, it's one of the biggest names in world football, so the challenges would be considerable. One of the best features about the club was the extensive archive it had stored on the database so, historical pieces such as past player interviews and footage were made far easier by that facility.

I am a people person so, having to conduct weekly interviews with the manager and first-team squad members came fairly easy to me.

I had the advantage of having worked for the club on a freelance basis for a number of years, prior to taking up the full-time position so I had established contacts within the organisation.

With relation to Morton – obviously a much smaller club but with the same challenges. Initially, I hosted the club's matchday hospitality on a freelance basis. In that capacity, I came to know the manager and players so, the transition to PR and Media, was made easier by that relationship. The job, again on a freelance basis, was divided into separate components.

The PR challenges in 2020/21 were the shutdowns due to the pandemic, the corrosive abuse of the club chairman by some individuals and the fact that, in a fraught battle against relegation (successfully navigated), the club employed three managers in one season.

In all situations, it was important to protect the club's integrity and position. There is a duty of care implied in the job and this applies, especially to the players. Footballers want to concentrate on training and the upcoming games and, in the main, are not enamoured by media duties.

I felt it was important to establish a bridge between the media, Press in particular, that ensured that journalists contacted myself first in relation to any interviews that they required.

In my view, there is nothing a player/manager hates more than a random phone call to set up an interview. I saw it as my job to take that burden away from them.

In addition, I established a presence online with a weekly video interview that involved either a player or part of the management structure.

This, I felt, was a vital point of contact between the club and their supporters. Equally, we were reaching out to paying customers and, in general, this was well received.

On a matchday, we would, as standard practice, put out a video on social media an hour before kick-off, that announced the team and any changes due to injury, etc.

This meant the support got that news directly from the club rather than mainstream media outlets.

In setting up the matchday livestream, I took the template of CelticTV and brought that to the club. The professionalism that went into that could not have been made possible without the dedicated team of experienced volunteers who bought into the concept and enhanced the production.

From the start we established a 'magazine' feel to the broadcast by going on-air approximately twenty minutes prior to kick-off and our pre-match show would involve analysis of the line-ups and interviews with a player and the manager. All of this was done in the company of former Morton great, Andy Ritchie whose contribution was professional, welcoming and entertaining.

At half-time, we would run highlights from a previous match, a Goal of the Month competition and then first-half analysis.

All in all, the production tied into the crucial lines of communication and contact between the club and their supporters which was equally true for Celtic and Morton.

You are also a successful author who has worked with high profile footballers to write their autobiographies including Packie Bonnar and Jackie McNamara. Can you sum up the creative process involved in producing and publishing a book on behalf of a high-profile individual?

For me, the most essential thing is to establish a relationship with your subject and then try and bring out the qualities that took them through their life and career.

After that, I feel it is essential to create a 'style' of writing that engages the reader. I have never been interested in writing a book just full of statistics about games or a mere chronology of a career. In that respect, I attempt to catch the reader right from the start of the book so that it pulls them in.

The individual is the key component in this process and must buy into the story and the style as well as be willing to let the reader inside the narrative.

Your success as a presenter, commentator and author has led to you hosting various 'Evenings with. . .' events with footballing personalities. How do you prepare for such events and what is the key to effectively hosting and comparing such an event in front of thousands of live fans?

In the professional life, 'preparation' is absolutely key to what I do, and this is especially true for live player events. It is crucial to know the individual and anticipate the areas of their career that they would like to discuss.

The most important thing for me is to engage with the individual and the audience.

The first thing is to get the audience on my side and I do that by the process of a short warm-up before bringing our guest out onto the stage. Then it's all about discussion. If you are going to make the individual feel comfortable then it's important to initiate conversation rather than a scripted interrogation. This sort of thing relaxes the individual and makes for a much better evening.

The audience should almost feel like they are sitting in a living room, listening to an interesting conversation rather than a show. I always believe in doing a Q&A session as well. This allows the audience to ask the questions that they would like to hear answers to as well as establishing an almost personal contact between them and the individual.

It would be arrogant for me to assume as a host that I have the sole privilege of asking the 'right' questions when the audience will have their own memories and narrative of that individual's career and life.

CHAPTER EIGHT
Producing the game

Jonny Owen
Football on film

Jonny Owen is an actor, producer, writer and director who has been involved with multiple award-winning football films, including *I Believe in Miracles and Don't Take me Home.*

You have produced award winning football films and documentaries in your career so far. The genre of sports documentary continues to grow year upon year. What have you made of the growth of football on film in your lifetime as whole and during your career in the industry?

I often say we are living in a real golden era of sports documentary filmmaking. I'm lucky enough to have got to know a lot of the directors and producers and they are all supremely talented. It's not just football either it's across all sorts, just recently you've seen the release of *The Three Kings*, which is all about the great middleweights of the 1980s. We're so lucky. I think the real turning point was *Senna*. In the sense that it showed there was a real appetite for this kind of film making. After that companies were more likely to invest in them. I really hope it continues.

You have produced films on Brian Clough, Jock Stein, Sir Matt Busby and Bill Shankly. All footballing immortals in their own right. What is the main aim that you set out to achieve when producing a film encompassing the life and achievements of a legendary figure?

I think at first, it's to tell their story from my perspective. That's all you can do really. It's your truth and hopefully people can see something of theirs in that. There's often a raft of books and films about these managers and so there's often nothing new for people but I think if you have a new perspective then that can make people want to see them. I was keen to do the films in a very modern way for a new audience. You sometimes have to remember that you are talking to people who maybe don't know what you'd assume they would. The Producers of *The Three Kings* were very keen that we made something for an 18-year-old to watch. Same with *I Believe in Miracles*, we wanted to cut the football to music in a very modern way. That often gives it a new life. It's one of the most pleasing things about it when someone young says how much they enjoyed.

Producing films such as I Believe in Miracles ***and*** The Three Kings ***must involve a lot of work. What kind of timescale do you set yourself for a project like those and how long does it take from idea for the finished product in your experience?***

It's usually about eighteen months. It can be longer or in the case or *Don't Take me Home* shorter (that's because we had to hit deadlines) but that's the rough timescale. The most time consuming is finding the footage and then putting it together. We often have to request access to old tapes and then go through it ourselves. It's great fun to do of course but very time consuming. Once you've got the basic material that you know you can work with then it's all about putting it together in the style you want and the music you'd like to use. Once you get near to completing then you have to get the original footage (they always send you temporary film) and start clearing the songs you'd like. After that it's all about getting the dates for release in the cinema or with the streamers.

Given the unscripted nature of sport and the stories that it continually provides year upon year, do you think that the rise of sports film and documentary making will only continue to grow in the decades to come?

Yes, I think it's an established genre now. People love them. *Last Dance* for instance was one of the documentaries of the lock down. I think because the stories are never ending, they will always stay with us now as a respected part of the art form. A good example would be Tyson Fury. In a few years that will make for one of the great sports stories. I hope more and more young filmmakers will keep exploring this style of storytelling. I know things date but hopefully they can look back at what people have been doing these last few years and be inspired by it and create their own style. That would be the best legacy of all.

CHAPTER NINE
Financing the game

Kieran Maguire
The Price of Football

Kieran Maguire is an academic, author and broadcaster. Maguire co-presents *The Price of Football* podcast and is the author of *The Price of Football.*

As football fans, we are often interested to know about the realities of our clubs financial state. What are the main aspects that contribute to the financial health of any football club?

Generating cash and controlling costs. Those are two crucial factors.

Whilst fans are often uncomfortable with the phrase 'monetisation', it helps pay the bills if the club can generate cash three hundred plus days a year by using the stadium for a variety of activities instead of the twenty to thirty days that the stadium hosts home fixtures.

Equally, being able to say no to wage and other demands from players and managers helps the long-term sustainability of a club.

The transfer window fascinates fans and pundits alike. Vast fees have become the norm at the top level of the game. How is a transfer typically funded – do clubs typically pay a transfer in full straight away?

A transfer can be funded on a one out, one in principle. However, these days most deals are on credit, with perhaps twenty per cent or more down payment and the remainder paid annually over contract period or shorter. This process is called amortisation. To give context to the use of amortisation, English Premier League clubs collectively owed about £1.5 billion in outstanding transfer fees at the end of the 21/22 season.

Over the last decade, historic clubs such as Bury FC and Macclesfield FC have been expelled from the EFL due to financial difficulties.

Is the elite game in danger of becoming almost a separate sport from the lower leagues and could independent regulation help avoid such a danger?

Most clubs are lost due to financial mismanagement, greed or lack of income. Legislating against this is difficult but not impossible, so whilst a regulator is a step in the right direction it is not a cure all.

You have taken football finance to the mainstream along with Kevin Day and Guy Kilty with The Price of Football *podcast. The show has been downloaded millions of times by fans across the globe. What are the key elements of the show, and have you and the team been shocked by the growth and demand of the show?*

Personally, I'm totally baffled about the success of the show. It has found a diverse audience (popular with club staff apparently) but we have tried to be true to the Reithian principles of inform, educate and entertain. Working alongside Kevin has been an eye opener for me, he is consummately professional as a presenter whilst playing the role of the Everyman in the pub who just wants to know a little more about the business side of the game. Similarly, producer Guy's background in broadcasting adds a sheen of professionalism to the final product.

I genuinely thought when we started it would last a month at most and we would fail to gel and run out of stories. Almost four million downloads later and a live show that has sold out has proven us wrong. I think listeners know we are authentic and there is a genuine respect and affection both within the team, but also to the game and fans, and that builds listener loyalty.

*****

Daniel Geey
Football and the law

Daniel Geey is a partner in the sports group at Sheridans, helping clubs and athlete with transfers and contracts. He is also the author of *Done Deal* and *Build the Invisible*.

You are a football lawyer. What does the role typically involve on a daily basis?

Since becoming a lawyer, I've been privileged to have worked on a number of high-profile football takeovers, transfers and disputes, meeting some fantastic people in the industry. The life of a football lawyer is, however, rarely glamorous. Deals can be finalised and photographed in the boardroom, but the nuts and bolts and the details are negotiated on WhatsApp, after mountains of emails, sometimes in the early hours of the morning and after forty calls to your client each day. I've had moments when I've helped a client negotiate a transfer while picking my kids up from school, or I have been on holiday and ended up working because the deal has been agreed in principle and the player was flying in the next morning. I've helped with deals on the beach, in the snow, on boats, and (losing signal) up mountains. Seldom are negotiations straightforward, as some may presume. But with email and smartphones readily available, there are rarely barriers to finalising a deal.

Kieran Maguire talked about the reality of financial management involved in a potential football transfer. What is the reality of the legalities that are involved in a transfer?

Transfers of elite players are usually highly complex. Agents, players, club officials, lawyers and accountants are usually all needed to complete high-profile deals. Everyone will be making compromises to get the deal over the line, sometimes at the very last minute. The crux of a deal is contained in the transfer agreement between the clubs and the employment contract between player and buying club. The array of clauses, stipulations and conditions can make for complex negotiations. The issue lawyers often encounter is trying to explain to their client (the club, player or agent) why negotiating on technical details of a particular clause is important. Usually, things work out fine, but lawyers especially are looking out for the situation where a player is sacked, money is not paid or obligations from either side are not fulfilled. My job is to manage that risk and communicate it as accessibly as possible. It's fair to say that the transfer fee headlines only usually provide a small glimpse into the nuances that make up a successful transfer and player contract negotiation.

You have negotiated numerous contracts across football over the year. Intriguing clauses have been reported in the press over the years. What are the strangest clauses that you can recall from your experience?

Although I'm not able to speak about particular deals I have been involved in, I talk in *Done Deal* about some amazing clauses that have been reported in the press over the years like:
• Sunderland inserting a provision that stopped their Swedish international footballer Stefan Schwarz from travelling into space.
• Arsenal legend Dennis Bergkamp, who has a fear of flying, insisting on a clause in his contract to ensure he was not forced to fly on away trips.
• When Rafael van der Vaart moved to Real Betis in 2015, it was reported that he could wear boots of any colour apart from red, the colour of Betis's local rivals, Sevilla.

Over the last few decades, football agents have become more prevalent in the modern game. There have been calls for caps on agent commissions and great regulation of the sector. What are agents usually like in your personal experience of working with them and which direction do you believe that the sector is heading in going forward?

From the public's perspective, being an agent is a glamorous, high-profile and highly lucrative profession for what some think demands very little work or effort. They are often seen as the curse of the modern game, the people responsible for driving transfer prices and wages up or down, depending on their client's priorities. However, agents are essential and play an important role in delivering the spectacle that is modern football.

There are plenty of extremely hard-working agents, who are paid very well and do a fantastic job for their clients. Now, it may sound simple enough to suggest that an agent gets a commission of five per cent or, if they are lucky, ten per cent. The difficult part to explain is usually who pays the agent. You'd think it would be the player, right? Wrong. It's the club and I think that if players paid their agents, just as athletes pay their agents in the US, for example, fans and wider stakeholders like FIFA would care less about regulating how much agents are paid.

There is big regulatory conflict on the horizon with the likely challenge of FIFA's proposed commission cap. FIFA argue that intermediaries are often paid too much and abuse their position in the market. FIFA as a result wants to cap player agent commission at a maximum of six per cent of a player's gross annual income. At the time of writing, pressure is mounting and it looks likely matters may end up in court in the future. It's getting close to injury time for both FIFA and the various agency representation groups to agree a capped compromise. FIFA's negotiating strategy with the master negotiators promises to make for an interesting few years ahead.

*****

Roger Mitchell
The future of football

Roger Mitchell spent fourteen years as the first CEO of the Scottish Premier League.

You were the Inaugural CEO of the Scottish Premier League (SPL) from 1998 to 2002 who was charged with establishing the highest profile sports organisation in the country. What did that role involve?

In my role at the SPL, I was responsible for all administrative, organisational and football issues. I was also involved with government and international sporting bodies on political and sport development aspects. Public facing PR duties was crucial to that too.

In addition to that, I had full involvement in all aspects of sports marketing, including rights management, direct negotiation and management of all broadcast media deals.

What would you pick out as being your favourite footballing memories from a personal and professional perspective?

From a personal perspective, I have four moments that come to mind right away. I would say Celtic's defeat of Barcelona in 2012. I went to the game with my son, who was ten years old at that time. It was his first game at Celtic Park and obviously, it became such an historic game for Celtic.

We were in hospitality and Celtic treated us very well and as such his memory of Celtic and that night is super positive.

I would also pick out the moments that I presented medals on the pitch when teams won the SPL. We had designed the trophy at the SPL, and it was very satisfying to be close to people in their moment of triumph. That was true for Rangers too, but it undoubtedly meant more when it was my own club, Celtic.

Seville was a great moment following Celtic. It was an astonishing day. A city was completely dominated by the Celtic support who all behaved beautifully. They changed the colour of the city from its norm and that is an image that will last long in the memory for me.

Being based in Italy, I would also have to pick out Italy's World cup win in 2006. I had just moved to Como, and I will never forget watching the semi-final against Germany. I have been very lucky to see a lot of football in my life but also, been unfortunate to see my team in decline since I was a teenager. I cannot say that I have enjoyed real glory, but I've enjoyed elements over it over the years and I am happy with that.

From a professional point of view, I would pick out two moments.

I was fortunate to work in Italian football on television

before it became very big in the late 1980s going into the 1990s. I was able to take camera crews into Milanello and other teams and follow the top teams and players up close. Those are great memories for me.

Running the SPL which was a new football league at the time was also a proud moment professionally. It was great to have twelve successful club owners and entrepreneurs listening to me and giving me respect and credibility. That was really satisfying and those first three years at the SPL were great. Unfortunately, it unrivalled in the last year with internal fighting between Celtic and Rangers and the other ten clubs of the SPL. It was difficult. However, I've always found that in football there are many people with serious brains and minds who have often done great things with their lives having come from nothing. I enjoyed working and hanging around with them.

Given your experience of leading a football league and working in finance for many years, what do you believe the future of football looks like?

Where is football going? I have been doing a podcast for years called *Are you not entertained?* that has been talking about where the game is going.

Football is heading into the polarisation of large, renowned clubs and smaller, community clubs. This theme of polarisation is what I like to call product market fit.

In my opinion, for younger generations, there is no market for a Motherwell vs Morton or a Crystal Palace vs Brighton. Those are products that do not have any real long-term future.

So, we are going to see modern football fandom at the top end polarising around twenty clubs – call that a Super League if you want – and the rest of football will then become a sort of arthouse industry full of respect that is valid and worthy. I honestly think that the idea that the smaller community clubs can stay in the same leagues as the globally renowned clubs is fanciful.

CHAPTER TEN
Following the game

Kevin Day
Travelling the country

Kevin Day is a stand up comedian, writer and sports presenter. He co-hosts *The Price of Football* podcast. He is also a lifelong Crystal Palace supporter.

You are an avid football fan who has also worked on footballing programming on television and radio. Therefore, what does football fandom and your beloved Crystal Palace mean to you?

I'm a very proud Londoner (I often wish I could put Londoner down as my nationality) but the area I'm from is kind of non-descript so for decades my entire identity has been sort of defined by Crystal Palace FC. I love the fact that some people will say 'oh yeah, you're a comedian' or 'oh yeah, you do that podcast' but most will say 'oh yeah, you're a Palace fan'. It actually makes me very proud that I'm associated with the club, especially now I'm a trustee of Palace for Life.

We recently launched a fundraising campaign called 'Made in South London' which has been incredibly successful because it taps into local pride that is hard to articulate in other ways. People expect Scottish people to be proud of Scotland and Welsh people to be proud of Wales and rightly so, but we are very proud of South London and it also ties in to the fact that pride in being English still carries negative connotations.

I think it's nigh on impossible for non-football fans to understand the bond you have with your club or the fact that I will get genuinely tearful in the Pawsons Arms on Boxing Day when I look around at all the Palace stuff on the walls and all the people I know and love through Palace.

And the older I get the less important the football becomes. I love the game so much but I've been in the third division with Palace and I was there when we ten minutes away from being liquidated, it's the community that matters more than the actual game.

Although, of course, there are so many happy memories that football has brought me, and some terrible ones!

I hope that makes sense.

As well as being a football fan, you have also worked within the game on shows such as Match of the Day 2. *What are your favourite memories over the years from a professional and personal perspective?*

MOTD2 was the best job I've ever had, I absolutely loved it, even when I was moaning about being driven home from Newcastle at three in the morning after covering a very rare Saturday night game.

I grew up loving *Match of the Day* so for me to actually be in a show that had that theme tune was real pinch-me stuff, and being pitch-side at Old Trafford or actually sitting in the dug-out with Harry Redknapp at Portsmouth was amazing.

The insight I got was incredible and some of the people I met even more so.

I suppose the highlights were getting the only interview with Sylvester Stallone at an Everton game because Bill Kenwright had told him I was working class, discussing socialism with Ricky Villa and Ossie Ardiles, and the entire away end of Man City fans at West Ham singing 'Kevin Day is a wanker' because I'd said something good about United the week before!

But it was meeting fans that was the most fun: travelling the country with generous, funny, intelligent people united by their love of the game. I think I got a bit of credibility through being a Palace fan: I supported my local team and we were shit at the time.

I particularly remember the Portsmouth fans who wouldn't say Harry Redknapp's name when he went to Southampton,

Swansea fans teaching me how to swear in Welsh and having really hot curry at a West Brom Baltic house. And I'm still really good friends with a posh lady called Eva, a Man City fan who apologised for the away end calling me a wanker and cheerfully admitted that she had joined in!

Based on the evolution of the game in your lifetime so far, what do you believe the future of football will look like?

Very interesting question! There is no doubt in my mind that nostalgic as all football fans are, things are much better now. The games are better, facilities and pitches are better, it's safer and the police treat us as human beings now (for the most part).

There has also been so much progress (but still not enough) around issues of racism, homophobia, etc.

However, much as I love hosting *The Price of Football*, the relentless bad news makes it difficult to be optimistic about the future of football as we know it for clubs outside the traditional top six.

I think a European Super League is inevitable. I think individual club broadcasting deals are inevitable which will concentrate the money even more to the big clubs. I genuinely fear that there will eventually be an attempt by US owners of English clubs to create a no-relegation Premier League which will take Government legislation to stop.

My real worry is that football will inevitably become too expensive for its traditional fan base. I already know people who simply can't justify the ticket price to their families with heating bills to be paid.

I'm not sure either, that a country the size of England can sustain a hundred and fifteen professional football clubs.

However, the game and its fans are resilient so we'll keep going to the pub to talk the same bollocks to the same people before watching a game somewhere even if, for most of us, it's in a league we can't possibly win.

*****

Pete Boyle
Following your team across the world

Manchester United superfan Pete Boyle has supported United since his first game in 1974.

You have followed Manchester United for decades. What are your favourite memories from your travels up and down the country following the side through thick and thin?

There's so many to choose from. My childhood was poor but happy and the 1977 FA Cup run was my reason for falling in love with the club. I went to my first game in November 1974 aged four years old but it's the '77 team which finally won me over.

I went to most of the cup run including the quarter-final, semi-final and the final itself when beat Liverpool to stop them doing the treble that we would achieve twenty-two years later.

I'm grateful to my late father for taking me at such a young age and I have done similar with my own son Georgie.

I loved all the decades following United even when the football wasn't great under Dave Sexton but it was still a thrill when the turnstiles open and you ran up the steps of the Stretford End and saw the pitch etc.

I remember under Ron Atkinson around Christmas and New Year. We played three home games in a week. I went to the Sunderland and West Bromwich Albion games which were both dour goalless draws. I couldn't go the Aston Villa game in between and yes, we won 3-1, typical.

The mid-eighties was a great time and some of the football was great. Trips to Wembley in '83 and '85 were particular highlights and in 1985-86 I finally thought I was going to see us win the league for the first time in my life but it wasn't to be.

I was actually gutted when Atkinson was sacked and I went to his last game on the Tuesday night at Southampton. I worked till one, I got the train to Euston, the tube to Waterloo and a train to Southampton. I had to leave at 3-0 down to get the train back to Waterloo and across to Euston.

I got back to Piccadilly at 3am and I was allowed to sleep on the train before I went straight into work at 6am.

In hindsight obviously replacing him for Fergie was clearly the right decision but I had enjoyed some great times watching Big Ron's United.

After a few dark years, generally we were obviously blessed with Fergie's football and success.

It's too hard to pinpoint a favourite memory from his days and lots say Rotterdam or the treble for obvious reasons. I will always be most grateful to the first ever title In 1993 because after 1985-86 and 1991-92 I honestly thought I'd never see us win the league.

Also the 1995-96 season is so special to become the first team to win the double twice and completing it by beating our biggest enemy with four minutes to go with a goal by Eric Cantona doesn't get any better and as a bonus City also got relegated.

The match going fans and social media followers of Manchester United can be completely different in terms of how they interact with each other. You have been openly critical of 'fan cams' and their 'influence'. Can you explain your views on this?

If we all thought the same, liked the same music, admired the same politicians and had the same favourite players life would be boring.

We've always had moaning fans, ones who know best, know more than the manager in their own opinion etc.

Fanzines were a labour of love compiled by match going fans to give an alternative view and as some had became a little bit successful, maybe as a bonus, subsidised them going to the game.

All of the fan cams I've come across are completely different and purely a business venture first and foremost, they are just giving the fans a voice and they are an alternative viewpoint.

The fact that most of people behind have seemingly just appeared out of nowhere in the last ten years, actually says a lot to me and many other fans.

It's about views and clicks and even subscriptions. The more outrageous and emotional rants on video the better for the ratings and ultimately more money.

There's absolutely nothing wrong in wanting a change of manager or wanting certain players selling or dropping but when the game is on and whilst they are playing or managing Man Utd I will support them unconditionally.

The fact that most of the people who called for fellow fans to demonstrate against Ole Gunnar Solskjaer (who's a club legend too) when he was manager are on social media behind fake profiles is a testimony to all that's wrong with the internet fans.

Fuelled by the fan cam and YouTube generation they are undermining any genuine Anti-Glazer movement and feelings and causing more divisions between fans.

I do not know one genuine fan who although they want a new manager would actually attend a protest calling for him to be sacked.

Last but not least, if you had the pick the ultimate Manchester United eleven of your lifetime who would you choose?

My best Manchester United eleven would be:

Peter Schmeichel

John Gidman   Martin Buchan   Nemanja Vidic   Denis Irwin

Paul Scholes   Roy Keane   Bryan Robson   Ryan Giggs

Eric Cantona   Jimmy Greenhoff

Substitutes:
Norman Whiteside, Ruud van Nistelrooy, Jaap Stam, Steve Coppell, Edwin van der Sar

Acknowledgements

I owe so many people a heartfelt thank you for helping to make this book a reality.

To all the contributors, I could not have made this project a success without your support and generosity with your time: Daniel Geey, Willie Morgan MBE, Norman Whiteside, Andreas Brehme, Shaun Maloney, Alan Mahood, Matt Le Tissier, Sammy McIlroy, Nigel Quashie, John McGovern, Ron Atkinson, Paul Tisdale, Dick Campbell, Csaba Laszlo, Martin O'Neill, Brian McDermott, Roy Hodgson, Craig Brown, Rene Meulensteen, Jonathan Gould, Gary Lewin, Les Ferdinand, Keith Hackett, Stuart Dougal, Oliver Kay, James Rowe, Craig Burley, Martin Tyler, Alan Smith, Jock Brown, Jeff Stelling, Mark Pougatch, Dan Thomas, Gerard McDade, Jonny Owen, Kieran Maguire, Roger Mitchell, Kevin Day and Pete Boyle.

To my editor at World of Football Index, James Nalton, for proofreading the short stories and interviews featured in this book.

Thank you to everyone at Morgan Lawrence, my publishers, who have helped me with this book: Mathew Mann, Barrie Pierpoint, Harry Worgan and Peter Andrews.

Thank you to Lee Clark for the amazing cover.

And, finally, thank you to the readers. I hope you have enjoyed the stories.

MY CHOSEN SPONSOR
Man On! Inverclyde

Man On! Inverclyde is a well-being and suicide prevention charity, seeking to achieve the following objectives.

To promote the advancement of mental health and relief of adults and children in Inverclyde and beyond through providing access to information, training, peer support groups, therapies and other relevant opportunities that will allow adults and children, that are affected by mental health illness to develop coping strategies, feel comfortable talking about mental health and live fulfilled lives.

To save lives and reduce the rate of suicide of adults and children in Inverclyde and beyond by preventing suicide, improving lives, providing a safe, comfortable place to talk, increasing social connectedness, bringing the community together, to introduce safe talking within the community, to provide suicide awareness, providing peer to peer support.

To advance education of young people and adults alike, in Inverclyde and beyond through the delivery of initiatives and programmes in the community by providing learning and/ or mental health awareness training in order to empower and increase emotional literacy.

To prevent or relieve poverty of adults in Inverclyde and beyond through empowering through the delivery of community initiatives, training, education, in order to increase capacity and employability skills and promote financial inclusion.

To provide recreational activities of adults in Inverclyde and beyond, by offering a range of activities and skills with the aim removing as many barriers as possible to provide opportunities by addressing disparities & reducing inequality and improving the conditions of life.

A percentage of the sale price from each copy sold will go to Man On! Iverclyde.

Thank you for your support.

MORGAN LAWRENCE
PUBLISHING SERVICES

The following books are available to purchase from
Morgan Lawrence and all major book retailers

"MINDING MY OWN FOOTBALL BUSINESS"
The inside story of Leicester City's success in the 90s
By Barrie Pierpoint
Leicester City's first Chief Executive
with Mathew Mann

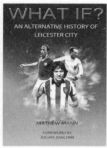

WHAT IF?
AN ALTERNATIVE HISTORY OF LEICESTER CITY
MATHEW MANN
FOREWORD BY JULIAN JOACHIM

"GIMME THE BALL"
MY TAKE ON THE BEAUTIFUL GAME
TERRY CURRAN
WITH JOHN BRINDLEY
FOREWORD BY RON ATKINSON

JULIAN JOACHIM
My Life In Football
YOU MUST BE JOACHIM

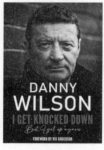

DANNY WILSON
I GET KNOCKED DOWN
But I get up again
FOREWORD BY VIV ANDERSON

THE SEAGULLS' BEST EVER SEASON
The incredible story of Brighton's 2022-23 season
TONY NOBLE
FOREWORD BY JOHNNY CANTOR

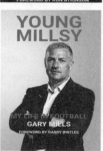

YOUNG MILLSY
MY LIFE IN FOOTBALL
GARY MILLS
FOREWORD BY GARRY BIRTLES

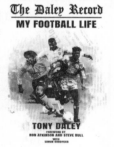

The Daley Record
MY FOOTBALL LIFE
TONY DALEY
FOREWORD BY RON ATKINSON AND STEVE BULL
WITH SIMON GOODYEAR

THE 100 CLUB
EVERY ONE FROM ARSENAL'S FIRST 100 CUP SCORERS
NICK BROWN
FOREWORD BY ALAN SMITH

THREE GAMES IN MAY
AND A TWENTY-YEAR ODYSSEY THAT DEFINED SIR ALEX FERGUSON'S MANCHESTER UNITED
ROB CARLESS
FOREWORDS BY STEVE BRUCE AND MIK CLISSE

INTRODUCTION BY GARETH SOUTHGATE
MALCOLM CHRISTIE
The Reality of the Dream
My unique journey from non-league to the Premier League
FOREWORD BY Steve McClaren & Steve Round
with Nathan Hunt

Here, There & Everywhere
THE GOOD, THE BAD & EVERYTHING IN BETWEEN!
SHAUN TEALE
FOREWORD BY BRIAN LITTLE
WITH ROB CARLESS

McMASTER & COMMANDER
THE BUSINESS OF WINNING
JOHN McMASTER

PENNY ELLIS
BIG BROTHER 2
Meet Me at the Mirror
Coping with reality.

David MacKinnon
Slide Tackles & Boardroom Battles
FOREWORD BY JOHN GREIG CBE

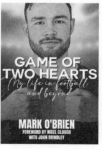

GAME OF TWO HEARTS
My life in football and beyond
MARK O'BRIEN
FOREWORD BY NIGEL CLOUGH
WITH JOHN BRINDLEY